Richard Kidder
World War II SURVIVOR

MANILA TO BATAAN.

TO CORREGIDOR.

TO CABANATUAN POW.

TO A HELL SHIP.

TO UMEDA BUNSHO POW IN OSAKA.

TO TSURAGA POW.

TO HOME, ALIVE. . .

✸ ✸ ✸

GORDON SAWYER

ISBN: 1-4196-8547-3

ISBN-13: 9781419685477

Visit www.booksurge.com to order additional copies.

PREFACE

It has been said that the United States of America was built by COMMON AMERICANS of UNCOMMON VALOR. Richard Kidder is one of these common but uncommon Americans. He did not come from Royal stock. He was not rich. He grew up in America's heartland, and was educated in public schools. He volunteered for service in the peacetime Navy as an enlisted man in 1936, during the depression. The U.S. Navy taught him a trade as a metalsmith, and in 1940 he was assigned to the Pacific Fleet.

When he found himself in a front row seat at the beginning of World War II, he unflinchingly did his duty to bring America through the most dangerous time in our nation's history. His is a story that needs to be told, if for no other reason than to remind us of the price others have paid so that the rest of us in America may live in freedom.

Richard Kidder was a Navy petty officer, a machinist, serving aboard a submarine tender stationed in the Philippines on America's "day of infamy." His ship was crippled by a Japanese bomb, but before Manila fell the crew managed to get it across Manila Bay to Bataan, where it served as a repair shop for the Army during the three months the "Battling Bastards of Bataan" held out. He escaped to Corregidor, the island fortress at the entrance to Manila Bay, where he was made a rifleman in the "Navy Battalion", living in a rocky foxhole for the 27 more days America held off the Japanese there. He faced the Japanese as they stormed that island until General Wainwright surrendered all troops in the Philippines. As a prisoner of war of the Japanese he survived Cabanatuan #3 prison camp in the Philippines; survived a Hell Ship ride to Japan; served on a forced-labor detail at Umeda Bunsho in Osaka, Japan, and finally as a POW slave laborer loading and unloading ships at Tsuraga, in the same industrial region of Japan where Hiroshima and Nagasaki are located.

For years after World War II he hesitated to talk openly about his experiences. He felt the sacrifices made by others, and especially those who lost their lives, should be highlighted … not his. It was a granddaughter who eventually got him to talk to a class in her school. And his wife in their retirement years encouraged him to write down some of his war-time memories.

So it should be of no surprise to you, and especially to the waning numbers of World War II veterans (who will understand how he feels) when I tell you he agreed to let me attempt to record his story in book form under one condition: "I don't want you to try and make me out a hero," he said. "I am a survivor, but not a hero."

So, I will do my best to tell his story as a good historian would present it, and I will let you, dear reader, decide where to fit him among the legion of "Common Americans of Uncommon Valor" who have handed us this great and unique nation we call the United States of America.

Gordon Sawyer
Gainesville, Georgia
2008

CONTENTS

Once home, with ample American food, good medical care and TLC (tender loving care) from family and friends, Richard Kidder recovered rapidly. The photograph on the next page was taken less than a year after his return to the United States.

Chapter 1

THE 1930s IN AMERICA'S HEARTLAND

The Missouri Pacific Railroad's main line trains from Little Rock to Monroe, Louisiana, came through McGehee, Arkansas, on a regular basis in the 1930s, running precisely on schedule, and sounding the whistle that made that long, low, soulful sound of the steam engine era. McGehee was a country railroad town, and the tracks split the community wide open, right down the middle. The railroad was important to the Kidder family, for Richard Kidder's father was a conductor on the line that ran through his home town. It was a steady job, and in the depression era, a job like that was both respected and coveted.

McGehee, in America's heartland, was anything but a coastal Navy town. Yet that was where this sailor-to-be, Richard Kidder, spent his boyhood years. If Norman Rockwell had painted one of his famous Saturday Evening Post covers depicting the heartland of America in the 1930s, in might well have shown some barefoot boys – Richard included – carrying fishing poles as they walked along the hot, dusty streets of McGehee on their way to the nearby creek.

For Richard Kidder there are fond memories – almost Tom Sawyer memories – of growing up in that small town. There were bittersweet memories, too, of times when adversity struck. His mother and father divorced in 1927, and Richard lived with his father. His sister, Helen, helped raise young Richard and his two brothers, A. J., just older than Richard, and Marvin, just younger. His mother and grandparents lived in the Little Rock area. There were a lot of family members around, 34 cousins in the general area.

The local school was small and in easy walking distance from the Kidder home. It was one of those classic community schools which gave its students a rock-solid basic education, but practically no special courses or activities. It did, however, have a football team. In those days every self respecting school in Arkansas, Oklahoma or Texas had a football team, and every self respecting boy who was a boy "came out" for the team, including Richard Kidder, one of the smallest boys. As a senior, he might have weighed 135 pounds if one included leather helmet, shoulder pads and cleated shoes.

His graduation class had 20 students, 10 boys and 10 girls, and everybody knew everybody. Which meant you couldn't get away with anything. It also meant Richard knew every job that might be available in town when he graduated, but getting a job at the height of the depression was not going to be easy in McGehee, Arkansas. He was barely 17 when he graduated, and he was faced with boys from classes ahead of him, even college graduates, who had returned to McGehee and taken menial jobs like driving milk trucks or bread trucks. It wasn't hard to see that the outlook was dim for new high school graduates who were less mature and less well educated. Thus it was that in June of 1936, Richard Kidder walked out to the side of the road going north, stuck out his thumb, hitch hiked up to Little Rock, and signed up for the United States Navy. After getting a problem with his birth certificate straightened out, he passed the mental and physical exams and was accepted. But – partly because of the depression – there was a long line ahead of him, and it would not be until November 13, 1936 that he was sworn in.

During this 6 month period, he worked very hard for little pay. Kidder tells it this way: Every week "I worked three jobs. On Mondays through Thursdays I drove for a Frigidaire dealer for 50 cents a day. On Wednesday and Sunday nights from 6 to 11 p.m., I was a 'soda jerker' in the ice cream parlor for 75 cents a night. On Fridays and Saturdays I worked in the Kroger store as an assistant to the butcher for the princely sum of two dollars a day. My hours on Fridays were from 7:30 a.m. until 6 p.m. and on Saturdays from 7:30 a.m. until about 1 a.m. Sunday morning. After closing on Saturday night we had to thoroughly clean everything before leaving. My total week's wages were $7.50 for all three jobs." In that economy the Navy was looking better and better.

Finally he came to the head of the line waiting to be inducted into the United States Navy, and on November 13, 1936, Richard Kidder went to Little Rock where he was sworn in.

Chapter 2

BELL BOTTOM TROUSERS, COAT OF NAVY BLUE

The United States Navy had a recruiting slogan that said "Join The Navy And See The World", and in Richard Kidder's case the Navy started paying off on this promise the day he was sworn in. After signing up in Little Rock, Kidder and about 15 other new recruits were put on a train and sent across the plains of the mid-west and over the Rocky Mountains to San Diego, California. For a Southern boy who had hardly been outside the state of Arkansas, it was an exciting start for a great adventure.

At the Naval Base in San Diego the recruits shed their civilian clothing, got a hair cut, and were issued a sea bag full of Government Issue Navy clothing. Packing a sea bag is like fitting a puzzle together; every piece of clothing has to be rolled tightly or the sailor will not be able to get all of his clothing in the confines of that heavy canvass bag. Richard Kidder remembers it this way: "We were issued our sea bag of clothing, our mattress, sheets (which fit over the mattress like a pillow slip), two blankets and of course our hammock. From our enlistment until the fall of Corregidor in May, 1942, every time I was transferred I had to pack my bag, roll it in the mattress and carry sea bag, mattress and hammock with me. I more or less lived out of my sea bag and either slept in my hammock or on a cot. Until World War II, if any of this initial issue of clothing (about $100 worth) wore out, it had to be replaced from our pay. It wasn't until World War II that clothing allowances were instituted. Needless to say, we learned early on to take good care of our clothing and to be frugal. Of course, we washed everything by hand. Would you believe that I still had some of my initial issue of clothing when war broke out five years later, in December, 1941?"

Navy Boot Camp is an intense three month training period in which civilians not only learn about service on a ship, but also learn the history and traditions of the United States Navy. Perhaps of more importance, it instills in the new recruits the discipline and teamwork required to go into battle, survive and win. The expectation in both the Navy and the Marine Corps is that the recruit will go into Boot Camp a boy, and come out a man.

When Seaman Kidder completed Boot Camp he scrounged up all the money he had, borrowed $10 from one of his new friends, and headed for home in Arkansas on a two week leave. This time he was riding a Greyhound bus, and again he was "seeing the world." There was, of course, excitement when this newly minted sailor came home; although, it was a different type excitement found around a returning World War II sailor, which Richard Kidder would experience – years later.

✧ ✧ ✧

One of the advantages of the peacetime Navy was that it taught many of its recruits a skill that could be used once they returned to civilian life, and on his return to San Diego Richard Kidder was aimed toward the engineering group, the section of the Navy that kept ships running and seaworthy. His specific assignment was to the Navy's metal school, located at the naval base at Norfolk, Virginia, and it brought about his first trip at sea. The Navy did not send their people across the United States by land at that time. They had two World War I vintage transports, ships that were slow but seaworthy, and as some pointed out, only 20 years old, for the First World War was not all that far away. Kidder was loaded on one of these ships, the USS Chaumont for his first trip through the Panama Canal and to Norfolk. It was on this first trip that Kidder learned he had an inner ear condition that would cause him to get sea sick, a problem he never conquered, and that dogged him throughout his Navy career. It was one of those things he simply "learned to live with."

He spent five months attending classes in a comprehensive metalworking course, a type of work he enjoyed and could do well. Upon completion he was loaded on the other slow transport, the USS Henderson, and sent back to San Diego for his first fleet assignment.

✫ ✫ ✫

Kidder was assigned to a destroyer tender, the USS Whitney. A tender is the "mother ship" for a group of fighting ships, in this case four to five destroyers. The "mother ship" is responsible for the "stores" required by the destroyers (except for fuel) such as food, ammunition and supplies of all kind.

The "mother ship" was also responsible for maintenance and repairs for all in its group, and this was the duty station assigned to Kidder on the Whitney, which had a well equipped metal working shop. He started as a metalsmith "striker" (an apprentice) in the copper shop.

Richard Kidder spent three years on the Whitney, helping repair destroyers and learning his trade. He became proficient at welding steel sheets with the torch, bending copper pipe to fit around the machinery in the engineering spaces of the destroyers, and shaping sheet metal.

He moved from Seaman 2nd Class to Fireman 3rd Class (same pay grade) because metalsmiths were in the engineering force and were promoted on the Fireman track, not the Seaman. While on the Whitney, he was promoted to Fireman 2nd Class, Fireman 1st Class, and Metalsmith 2nd Class, the rating he held when he was transferred from the Whitney in January, 1940. The promotions also had a favorable effect on his income. His boot camp pay was 21-dollars a month. Seaman 2nd Class and Fireman 3rd Class 36-dollars a month. In the next five years, as he was promoted up the ladder, pay increases took him to 54, 60, and 72-dollars per month. When the war broke out he was a Petty Officer First Class (first class Metalsmith) earning $84 a month. Manpower is essential in any military force, but in the Navy a fully operational ship is essential, and Richard Kidder's skills at keeping a ship operational were highly prized.

It was in 1939 that his mother and sister, Helen, moved from Arkansas to California. Richard Kidder enjoyed having family in the area, and although they were in Los Angeles and he was in San Diego, he was able to visit with them before leaving for the Philippines. He bought a used 1934 Ford coupe for 95-dollars and left it for his mother to use, which she did throughout World War II.

The three years in which Richard Kidder was stationed on the Whitney were very pleasant. Most of the time the ship lay at anchor in San Diego Bay, going to sea just often enough to keep the crew's seagoing skills sharp, and to make life interesting. The ship participated in some naval war games in the Carribbean, which necessitated another round trip through the Panama Canal. There were maneuvers around the Hawaiian Islands. The most enjoyable activity came when the Whitney went to San Francisco in the summer of 1939. A World's Fair was underway, and Petty Officer Richard Kidder remembered it this way: "Every chance I got I went to the Fair and listened to the free concerts by Benny Goodman and his orchestra. Ziggy Elman, who wrote 'And The Angels Sing' was the trumpeter for the orchestra. Ziggy played this song on his trumpet and sang it at every performance. It was something. I also saw 'Gone With The Wind' at the Fox Theater."

The years on the Whitney with San Diego as the home port were very pleasant duty "…except for the period in which I had to work as a mess cook, serving food and cleaning up after more senior sailors (the Army would call this KP). I had two three-month stints of this. I did learn how to wash loads of dishes and scrub floors. Mess cooking was hard, boring work."

✧ ✧ ✧

In the midst of all the storm clouds of war in Europe, in January of 1940, Richard Kidder set out for his new duty on the Navy's Asian Station, where things appeared to be more peaceful. Prior to World War II, the Navy did not rotate ships with the crew intact, as they did later and do now. The Navy in 1940 kept the ship on station and sent the new personnel to that ship, no matter where it was. Kidder's ship was at a port in China. It was "Join the Navy and See The World" all over again.

Let him tell the story: "I was first transported by ship from San Diego to Long Beach, California. Here I bunked on a ship for a few days until another ship came by sailing to Mare Island Naval Shipyard (in San Francisco). I finally got to Mare Island and spent some time there at the Receiving Station waiting for the USS Henderson, the other World War I transport that the Navy had at that time. It finally came in and was duly loaded with its passengers – sailors, Marines, and quite a few dependents. We set sail for the long journey to the Far East."

The transport operated like a "local" trolley, stopping along the way to deliver and receive personnel who were being transferred to and from each port. The first stop was in Honolulu, and that was the only port where Kidder was given liberty. He went ashore and remembers taking a tour of the island of Oahu, his first encounter with the beauty of the South Pacific. The transport stopped at Guam, and then Manila where he expected to find his new duty station, the USS Canopus, but that ship was in northern China, so they sailed on. They sailed up the Yangtze River to Shanghai, where the ship spent the night. "I would like to have had liberty there," Kidder said, "but no such luck. I can say that I have been to Shanghai, but not that I have visited it." They sailed on to Tsingtau, China, where Richard Kidder finally caught up with his new duty ship, the USS Canopus. Kidder had left the United States in January, and arrived at his new duty station half way around the world in May, 1940.

Tsingtau was a beautiful city, a chapter of German colonial history dating from 1897 to 1914. It was a unique introduction to the culture and the architecture of a German city in the Orient. Richard Kidder remembers it this way: "It was a really pretty city, with large, fine, brick German buildings and beautiful wide boulevards." Tsingtau was located just south of the point where the Great Wall of China reached the Yellow Sea. It was easy living for a sailor on the Canopus. Enlisted personnel had what was called "court martial" liberty from 1 p.m. until 8 p.m., just enough time to drink too much. Very often returning liberty parties were a rowdy, noisy bunch. Officers could stay overnight in a lovely, large hotel converted into an officers' club.

Tsingtau was in a part of China that had been occupied by the Japanese in January, 1938. The Canopus was anchored in the bay, and Kidder says: "I remember having to go through Japanese guards on landing and returning to our ship." Japan still had an embassy in Washington, and although there were serious disagreements between Japan and the United States, Japan did not deny the American Navy access to the port at Tsingtau. All told, Kidder's first few months on the Canopus were very pleasant, almost a summer vacation. But as the summer ended they lifted anchor, and set sail for their home port in Manilla, Philippine Islands.

✼ ✼ ✼

Richard Kidder was a long way from home as he sailed into Manila Bay. The Philippine Islands formed the westernmost United States military outpost, and for the most part it stood among islands that were controlled by other nations, including Japan. Pearl Harbor was 5,000 miles to the east; San Francisco 7,000. By contrast, Formosa, which had been under Japanese control since 1895, was just 200 miles North of the Philippine Island named Luzon, in easy flying range of the Philippines. Tokyo was only 1,800 miles from Manila.

The United States had maintained military forces in the Philippine Islands since their annexation in 1898. At the Washington Naval Treaty in 1922 the United States had asked for limitations on Japanese shipbuilding, and in return had agreed to stop building any new fortifications in its Pacific possessions. Then the United States had passed an act to grant the Philippines commonwealth status in 1935, and independence by 1946.

The new Philippines General Assembly had passed a National Defense Act in 1935, and General Douglas MacArthur had, after his retirement as Chief of Staff of the U.S. Army in 1937, come to the Philippines to advise the new government on defense.

USS CANOPUS — Kidder's ship prior to the outbreak of World War II. This submarine tender did not have the appearance of a military ship.

Kidder's ship, the USS Canopus, was built in 1919 for the merchant service. It had been acquired from the Grace Line in 1921, and converted into a tender with forges, machine shops, oil tanks and "other vitals necessary for her trade." She was named Canopus for the third brightest star in the night-time sky, and for 20 years had been the mother ship to American submarines in the Asiatic Fleet, mostly World War I "S" type boats that needed a good deal of maintenance. The Asiatic fleet was the last to get the newer ships, probably because of the Washington decision to give priority to the European theater, and the fact that German U-boats were creating havoc in the Atlantic. For Richard Kidder, things were relatively quiet for the rest of 1940 and most of 1941. Some of the new Squalus type submarines arrived, and the Canopus went to sea for some war games.

Manila was historic, but not a good liberty town. Kidder had this to say about it: "One quickly tired of walking about seeing sights and trying to absorb a foreign culture. Beyond that there was little for young sailors to do except go to bars and drink. When I enlisted in the Navy I was dead set against drinking, for my dad drank too much." When Kidder tried to keep up with his shipmates in Manila, which he did at times, "it almost always made me sick."

The sailors did, however, find a pleasant way to spend their liberty time on shore. Some of the sailors from the Canopus and some from the USS Blackhawk, a destroyer tender, rented the upstairs of a spacious home from a delightful, elderly Spanish lady. She kept the downstairs for her son and his family, and herself. "The upper level which we rented had a veranda running around it on three sides" Kidder said. The lady of the house treated her Navy renters like family, and they came to love and respect her.

She had a lovely six or seven year old granddaughter who could already speak four languages fluently: English from school; Spanish from home; and two Philippine dialects. "She rented the rooms four sailors to a room," Kidder recalls, "and I don't remember a time when all four sailors who shared my room were on liberty the same weekend." It was a wonderful break from the intensity that was building up in the military in the Philippines … a restful interlude that this group of sailors cherished.

The view from Manila was spectacular. Looking due west one immediately saw Manila Bay, and beyond that the Bataan Peninsula, and beyond that the South China Sea. Looking a bit to the southwest, across the bay, was the Corregidor Island fortress guarding the entrance from the South China Sea to Manila Bay. Looking almost South, and just a bit to the west, was a land mass, part of Luzon island, and the town of Cavite, the location of a U.S. Navy shipyard. It was an area with a lot of history, and a part of that history was a belief from many sailors who had come here over the centuries, that Manila had the most beautiful sunsets of any place on earth.

Corregidor was strategically located at the mouth of the Bay and had played a major role in many historic Philippine events. It was shaped like a giant tadpole with a high solid rock head and a long tail that curled out into the bay. It was perfectly located to defend Manila, and after the American Admiral, George Dewey, defeated Spanish forces in the Spanish-American War, and the United States gained control of the Philippines, Corregidor became a U.S. Military reservation. The Washington Naval Treaty apparently did not cover improvements to existing military installations, so in 1922 the Army started construction on a fortification that, at the time, was the wonder of the world.

Called the Malinta Tunnel, it was a tunnel through the solid rock of the "head" of the tadpole island. The tunnel was 835 feet long, 24 feet wide, and 18 feet high at the top of the arch. But that was just the beginning. There were 13 lateral tunnels on the north and 11 lateral tunnels on the South sides of the Malinta Tunnel, each 15 by 15 feet and 160 feet long. Inside, the tunnel had room for troop billeting, command and communications headquarters, and munitions storage, not to mention a 1,000 bed hospital. It was huge, and considered totally impregnable. The entire fortress was an amazing feat, especially since building the Malinta Tunnel was done at a time when Congress was allocating very little money for the military.

It was obvious to Richard Kidder that a large military build-up was taking place in the Philippines. This was the kind of "show of force" that had been a trump card in world diplomacy for centuries. When the ships of a major power showed up on the horizon, serious talks began. If the weaker nation perceived that the dominant player would use their military power, the dispute was almost always settled at the negotiation table.

Throughout the Pacific, the preponderance of thinking was that the war in Europe would not spread into the Far East. After all, who in his right mind would believe Japan would attack the powerful United States of America?

Chapter 3

CHURCHILL CALLED IT

"THE GATHERING STORM"

In Europe, Winston Churchill would call it "The Gathering Storm." In America we followed "The Winds of War." But whatever it was called, the war in Europe was the main feature among Americans, and Japan was an afterthought. A diplomatic problem, maybe, but not a serious military threat.

Trouble with Germany had started hardly a decade after the end of World War I, the "war to end all wars", when, in 1933, the Nazi Party came to power. Adolf Hitler proclaimed the Third Reich and became its dictator. In 1938, Germany occupied Austria. Britain and France threatened Hitler, but did not act. He then threatened Czechoslovakia, negotiated for some of its territory, and in March, 1939, Germany seized the rest of Czechoslovakia, and turned its attention to Poland.

Benito Mussolini, the Italian Fascist dictator, had invaded Ethiopia, in Africa, in 1935. Japan had occupied Manchuria in 1931, and started a war with China in 1937. In 1935 a Rome-Berlin alliance was announced, and then the "Axis" was formed including Germany, Italy and Japan. In the mid-1930's the

Western Powers considered Italy and Japan to be second rate powers, and Germany ... which had been decisively defeated less than two decades earlier in World War I ... to be too economically weak to pose a threat.

Hitler introduced the Blitzkrieg, and with a new generation of tanks on the ground, and the Luftwaffe in the air, rolled through Poland in late 1939. Norway and Denmark capitulated to Germany in April of 1940. The Netherlands, Belgium and Luxembourg fell in May.

German forces broke through the famed French Maginot Line, and on June 14, 1940, the French (as Hitler had predicted) surrendered, and set up the Vichy government controlled by Hitler.

The British had troops on the continent, fighting Germany, when France capitulated, but were able to evacuate their forces to England in a heart-rending volunteer "boat lift" from Dunkerque. They were forced, however, to leave most of their equipment behind. At that point, only the island nation of Great Britain stood between Germany and the United States.

The rapid defeat of France, and the possible collapse of Britain, created great concern in the United States, but not enough to enter a war that was "way off" in Europe, or a scuffle "way off" in the Far East. The U.S. Congress, led by anti-war and isolationist representatives and senators, had passed a Neutrality Act in 1937 which made it illegal for Americans to trade with belligerents. And President Roosevelt had campaigned on a "He Kept Us Out of War" platform in the election of 1940.

But the lightning victories by Germany caused the U.S. Congress to repeal most of the Neutrality Act, and to pass a "Lend-Lease Act" which gave the president authority to sell, transfer or lease war goods to countries when it was deemed vital for the defense of the United States. President Roosevelt declared that America would become the "Arsenal for Democracy". But just in case America "had" to enter the war, the first peacetime draft in American history (the Selective Service and Training Act) was instituted.

Because of the "Axis" alliance between Germany and Japan, especially after France and the low countries of Europe fell, there was growing concern that colonial holdings such as French Indo-China and the Dutch East Indies, plus others, might truly become "Japanese protectorates", which Japan was already claiming.

✢ ✢ ✢

The opinion in the western world was that the Japanese were a problem, but not a serious military threat. Japan was viewed as a backward island nation, with few resources. It was stymied without outside sources of coal, oil, even food. In attempting to secure more resources it had invaded China, an invasion that appeared to be stalemated. The common opinion among western powers was that Japan's China adventure was "too big a bite to swallow."

Great Britain had a strong military presence in the region: the impregnable fortress at Singapore, plus Hong Kong and other power positions. Britain's Far East Naval force was considered the strongest in that area, and despite that country's perilous position in Europe, it had just reinforced its naval forces in the South China Sea.

The United States had a solid Army presence in the Philippines. The Army Air Force had recently stationed 35 of the new "Flying Fortress" bombers at Clark Field, north of Manila, and there were more than 100 P-40 fighters there and at Ibo, farther North on the Philippine island of Luzon. The P-40's had gained a solid reputation as a leading fighter plane by the Flying Tigers, who flew them against Japan in China. A new Philippine military force was being trained by General MacArthur. And if all that wasn't enough, there was always the United States battleship fleet at Pearl Harbor, in Hawaii.

The U.S. Navy commanders in the Asiatic sector were getting the same vibes out of Washington as the military commanders at Pearl Harbor and General MacArthur in the Philippines – Japan could create problems, but they could be handled. But Admiral Thomas C. Hart, commanding Far East naval forces from Manila, was not as comfortable with his situation as Washington. Looking down on his sparse fleet from the North was the Japanese Imperial Navy with 10 battleships, 39 heavy or light cruisers, nine aircraft carriers, 113 destroyers, 63 submarines and hundreds of aircraft.

Admiral Hart was to cover the entire western Pacific with three cruisers, 13 over-age destroyers, a number of small gunboats, 30 "slow, cumbersome" PBY reconnaissance planes, six PT boats, and his strongest force, 29 submarines along with their tenders, the Canopus, Holland and Otus … and one small submarine rescue vessel, the Pigeon. The British had the strongest allied naval units in the region, and this force had just been bolstered with two new, powerful capital ships operating out of Singapore, the Prince of Wales and the Repulse.

In the face of these odds, if and when war did come, existing naval forces in the Far East were getting "ship shape." The Cavite Naval Yard was filled with ships and submarines getting final fittings and repairs. The submarine tenders – Canopus, Holland and Opus – had been working "on the double" dispersing torpedoes and ammunition. Several submarines had already been readied for combat and sent to assigned patrol stations that would allow them to inform U.S. forces about Japanese fleet movements.

This is not to say the U.S. Navy expected a massive attack the weekend of December 7, 1941 (December 8 in the Philippines), but they were well along toward getting prepared for whatever might come. The Canopus, with its submarines ready for action, was in Cavite Naval Yard for some small repairs while some of its crew were given a relaxing weekend pass.

✳ ✳ ✳

With this analysis of the situation in the Far East, Australia had sent several thousand of its best troops to fight alongside the British in North Africa.

It was obvious the United States and Great Britain felt they held a strong position in the Far East. They would use diplomacy and blockades, if necessary, to neutralize Japan in that part of the world while they focused their power against the serious threat in Europe.

✳ ✳ ✳

The Japanese saw it differently. The Center of Military History of the U.S. Army, in its 50th anniversary of World War II publications, summarized the Japanese viewpoint this way:

"Japan, largely devoid of natural resources to feed its industries, looked overseas for supplies of strategic materials such as ores and petroleum. Before 1939 the United States was Japan's major supplier. But President Roosevelt and Secretary of State Cordell Hull shut off American supplies in an effort to force the Japanese to end hostilities against China. The Japanese had long coveted the resource-rich British and Dutch colonies of Southeast Asia, and as the U.S. trade embargo tightened, the Japanese increasingly looked southward for raw materials and strategic resources."

"Only the United States stood in Japan's path. The U.S. Pacific Fleet at Pearl Harbor was the only force capable of challenging Japan's navy, and American bases in the Philippines could threaten lines of communications between the Japanese home islands and the East Indies. Every oil tanker heading for Japan would have to pass by American-held Luzon. From these needs and constraints, Japan's war plans emerged."

The war plan came to be known as Japan's "centrifugal strategy". With one massive and unexpected series of blows Japan would cripple America's naval power at Pearl Harbor and Manila. At the same time it would destroy the U.S. Army's air power in the Philippines. America's central Pacific bases at Guam and Wake would be seized. The Japanese army would begin to circle the western Pacific, taking Burma, Malaya, Singapore, and the Dutch East Indies. Germany would pressure already conquered European nations to assign their Far East colonial holdings as "protectorates" of Japan. The circle would be closed by taking islands in the South Pacific, isolating Australia and denying the U.S. any bases west of San Diego, on the American mainland. (See map at the end of this chapter)

The Japanese plan called for this to be accomplished in 90 days, well before the American battleship navy could recover and return to action in the Pacific.

Japan still had an embassy in Washington, D.C., and its ambassador had been reporting to Japan about the political turmoil in the United States. There was a powerful and very active anti-war movement. President Roosevelt had been re-elected on a strong "he kept us out of war" platform. The peacetime draft had been extended, but by only one vote in Congress. The U.S. had agreed to become the "Arsenal of Democracy", using our industrial might to arm others, but not to send troops. And it was obvious President Roosevelt's attention was focused on Europe.

Said the U.S. Center of Military History: "Japan's leaders were convinced that Americans, once involved in the European war, would be willing to negotiate peace in the Pacific."

✳ ✳ ✳

Looking back at the history of World War II, it now seems clear the United States firmly believed it could neutralize Japan through negotiations and embargoes, and that the Japanese military was not a serious threat to the United States.

Thus it was that the top American military commanders at Pearl Harbor were looking forward to a leisurely game of golf on Sunday, December 7, 1941, and at the same time in the Philippines, Navy Petty Officer Richard Kidder was enjoying a weekend leave in Manila while his ship, the USS. Canopus, was undergoing minor repairs at Cavite Naval Shipyard.

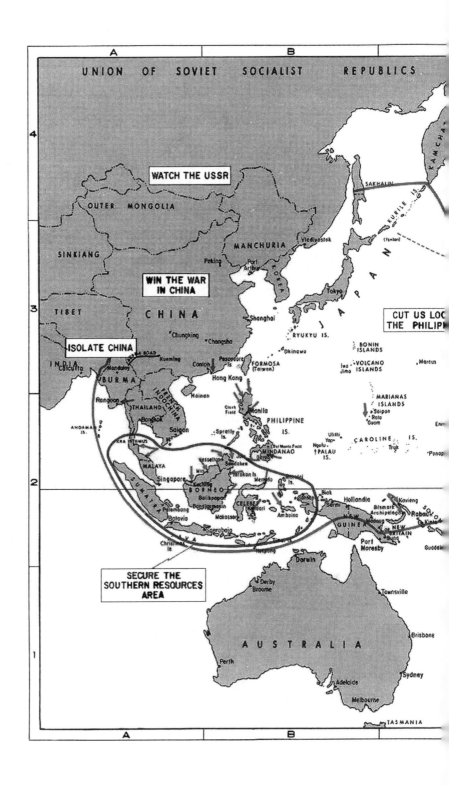

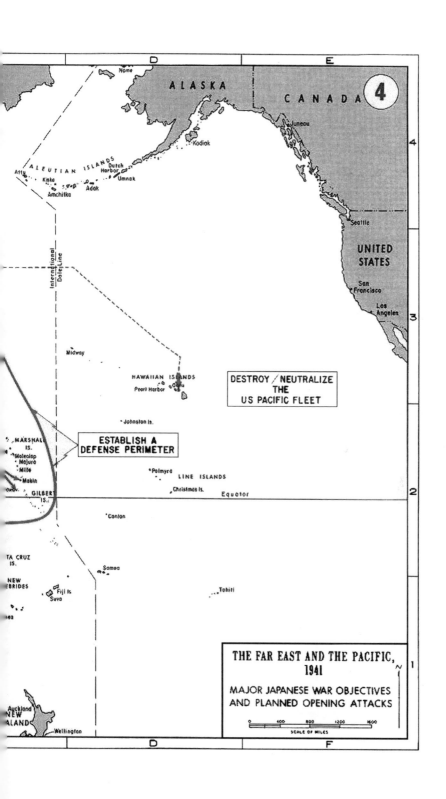

ALASKA

CANADA **4**

Nome

Juneau

Kodiak

ALEUTIAN ISLANDS
Attu
Kiska
Amchitka
Adak
Dutch Harbor
Umnak

Seattle

UNITED STATES

San Francisco

Los Angeles

International Date Line

Midway

HAWAIIAN ISLANDS
Pearl Harbor
Oahu

DESTROY / NEUTRALIZE
THE
US PACIFIC FLEET

Johnston Is.

MARSHALL
IS.
Maleolap
Majuro
Mille
Makin
GILBERT
IS.

ESTABLISH A
DEFENSE PERIMETER

Palmyra   LINE ISLANDS
Christmas Is.   Equator

Canton

TA CRUZ
IS.

NEW
EBRIDES

Samoa

Fiji Is
Suva

Tahiti

THE FAR EAST AND THE PACIFIC,
1941

MAJOR JAPANESE WAR OBJECTIVES
AND PLANNED OPENING ATTACKS

0   400   800   1200   1600
SCALE OF MILES

Auckland
NEW
ZEALAND
Wellington

Chapter 4

FIGHTING THE JAPANESE –

MANILA AND BATAAN

The book on Submarine Operations in World War II, written by Theodore Roscoe, says it was just before dawn on December 8, 1941, (in Manila) ".... When Canopus suddenly fractured the calm with a flashing message from her searchlight: FROM COMMANDER ASIATIC FLEET ... TO ASIATIC FLEET ... URGENT ... BREAK ... JAPAN HAS COMMENCED HOSTILITIES ... GOVERN YOURSELVES ACCORDINGLY." The Japanese had launched their "day of infamy" at Pearl Harbor, and the communications section of the Canopus was first to relay the message to all U.S. Navy ships in Manila Bay.

Richard Kidder and some of his shipmates were on a restful weekend leave and had spent the night at the home in Manila where they rented rooms. The Spanish lady who rented them the upstairs of her home usually fed them a leisurely breakfast before they left, and she had been listening to the radio that morning while preparing their food. She was the one who awakened Kidder and told him, and the other sailors, that the Japanese had attacked Pearl Harbor. It jolted them awake, and they left immediately, without eating.

With the Canopus at the Cavite Naval Shipyard Kidder grabbed a taxi cab and headed for his ship. The news of the attack had reached the Navy yard, and Kidder recalls there was utter confusion. "We had to stand around on the dock until yard workmen could hastily complete their work and inspection. When we were all aboard, we got under way, sailed across Manila Bay and tied up at one of the civilian piers in Manila. Moving to Manila was a wise move because on Wednesday morning Japanese bombers flew from Formosa and literally leveled the shipyard. There were no buildings left standing." The other submarine tenders, Holland and Otus, were ordered to move south to the Malay Barrier, and were able to escape with a convoy of merchant ships.

For the next few days there were Japanese air raids in Manila, although no bombs were dropped anywhere near the Canopus. But the fact things were relatively quiet in Manila certainly did not mean things were quiet on other fronts. In fact, even though the sailors on the Canopus had little time to absorb the "big picture", they did know things were not going well for the U.S., and that Japanese attacks were moving with astonishing rapidity.

✵ ✵ ✵

On the 50th anniversary of victory in World War II, the Army published a series of booklets describing that massive war. The publication describing the various battles in the Philippines had this to say about the first days of the war:

"By 1 December the Philippine Islands boasted the largest concentration of U.S. Army aircraft outside the continental United States. Many of these aircraft were the best the Army had to offer, including 107 P-40 fighter aircraft and 35 B-17 Flying Fortress bombers." The Army report states that nine hours after the attack on Pearl Harbor, Japanese aircraft "...caught two squadrons of B-17s lined up on (Clark) field and a number of American fighters just preparing to take off. The first wave of 27 Japanese twin-engine bombers achieved complete tactical surprise and destroyed most of the American heavy bombers. A second bomber strike followed while Zero fighters strafed the field. Only three P-40s managed to take off. A simultaneous attack on Ibo Field in northwest Luzon was also successful; all but two of the 3d Squadron's P-40s were destroyed. The (American) Far East Air Force lost fully half its planes the first day of the war."

After the successful destruction of the Cavite Naval Yard by the Japanese, most of the American Asiatic Fleet was withdrawn from Philippine waters, leaving only the Canopus and some submarines to contest Japanese superiority. But most of the submarines, without fully supplied "mother ships", were severely limited in range and ability to operate in Japanese controlled waters.

With air and naval superiority ensured, the Japanese started landings on small islands north of Luzon on 8 December, 1941. On 12 December Japanese troops landed on Southern Luzon and on 22 December the main attack began with Japanese troop landings on Luzon's Lingayen Gulf.

✳ ✳ ✳

American troops in the Philippines, along with the people at home in America, were being hammered with bad news.

...December 7, 1941 – the destruction of the fleet at Pearl Harbor. 21 warships out of action (including the sinking of the battleships Arizona and Oklahoma); 169 aircraft demolished; 2,403 Americans killed.

...December 8–9, 1941 – the destruction of air power in the Philippines. All of the B-17s destroyed at Clark Field. 102 of the 107 P-40 fighters disabled at Clark and Ibo Fields.

...December 9, 1941 – Cavite Naval Yard, on Manila Bay, bombed to oblivion with 1,400 casualties.

...December 10, 1941 – Japanese invasion forces take Guam and the Gilbert Islands.

...December 10, 1941 – Japanese bombers find Britain's new battleship cruisers Prince of Wales and Repulse at sea east of Singapore without air cover, and sink them both.

...December 21, 1941 – Siam (Thailand) becomes a Japanese protectorate – a political victory handed Japan by German victories in Europe. Japanese troops move in without opposition.

...December 22, 1941 – Wake Island is captured by the Japanese.

...December 26, 1941 – Hong Kong, Great Britain's trading port with China, is occupied by the Japanese.

...December and January – The Japanese take the Malay states, Sumatra and most of Borneo, as well as several of the Solomon Islands.

...February 15, 1942 – Singapore, the supposedly unconquerable British bastion on the tip of the Malay Peninsula, falls. At the same time the Japanese successfully move forces into Thailand and Burma.

The Japanese-based propagandist, Tokyo Rose, whose radio broadcasts were in English and who drew G.I. listeners in the Pacific by playing popular American music, played a rendition of the hit song "It's Three O'clock in the Morning" and jeered: "Where is the United States fleet? I'll tell you where it is, boys. It's lying at the bottom of Pearl Harbor."

If one combined the Pacific news with the news from Europe, it was obviously a dark and dangerous time for the entire free world.

✳ ✳ ✳

Back in the Philippines, where an American troop consolidation was taking place on Corregidor Island, Richard Kidder was part of a small group of metalsmiths and shipfitters loaned to the Army to build various metal equipment on Corregidor, mostly metal troughs to be used as outdoor latrines. They were crude with absolutely no privacy, he recalled, "but they did the job." After completing the task he asked to be returned to his ship. "I was afraid if I stayed there I would get tunnelitis." The massive Malinta Tunnel through sheer rock on Corregidor was a perfect shelter from the frequent Japanese bombings that hit that fortress island, and there was a tendency among troops to do whatever work they could in the safety of the tunnel. "Tunnelitis" was Kidder's term for that natural inclination, since Japanese bombers made frequent visits and anyone outdoors knew he was in harm's way.

"When I got back to my ship I found that in my absence the Manila waterfront had been bombed and the Canopus had received a direct hit in the shaft alley. The shaft alley is a small tunnel through which the propeller shaft connects the engines to the propeller. The blast severely damaged the shaft, all the spaces immediately above, and was sufficient to prevent our going to sea. We could get underway okay, and limp along, but we would have been sitting ducks on the high seas." Although there were intermittent bombings of Manila, the Canopus stayed dockside there for most of the rest of December without further damage.

The Japanese invasion force which had landed on northern Luzon was pushing relentlessly south toward Manila. Another Japanese force was moving toward Manila from the south. In late December, 1941, the Americans abandoned Manila, declared it an "Open City", and withdrew all forces toward Bataan, the peninsula across the bay. Everyone realized, Kidder recalled, that it was "hold here or else." On January 1, 1942, America's Asiatic submarine force was ordered to Java. Left behind, the Canopus limped across Manila Bay to the Bataan peninsula, and tied up in a sheltered cove named Mariveles Bay.

In early January Japanese airmen spotted the Canopus, and hit her directly amidships, at the smokestack, with a fragmentation bomb. The explosion made a shambles of the upper decks and caused 15 casualties. The battered ship was listing badly. The Canopus had become a repair facility for the army the moment she arrived on the tip of the Bataan peninsula, and it was quickly decided if she were to continue that role, the crew had to make her look like she was disabled and abandoned. The hope was that the Japanese would not think she was worth another bombing.

The captain of the Canopus, E. L. Sackett, explained it this way in a later biographic article: "The next morning, when 'photo Joe' in his scouting plane came over, his pictures showed what looked like an abandoned hulk ... from which wisps of smoke floated up for two or three days. What he did not know was that the smoke came from oily rags in strategically placed smudge pots, and that every night the 'abandoned hulk' hummed with activity, forging new weapons for the beleaguered forces of Bataan".

As Richard Kidder remembers it: "The Canopus was anchored close enough to the front lines that we could hear the boom of the big guns, even though we could not see the action. Everyone except a few essential personnel was removed from the ship, and set up camp in a rock quarry a mile or so away." The repair shop on the Canopus suddenly became an integral part of the "Battling Bastards of Bataan." The crew of the Canopus soon learned about short rations, constant shelling, lack of medical supplies, and how the seething heat could quickly drain all energy from an individual. Even so, Kidder makes it clear the life of the Canopus crew was better than that of the ground troops facing the Japanese in the hills of Bataan. For instance, he says, there was the ice cream machine. It had escaped damage from the bombs, and the storage area holding the ice cream powder had not been destroyed. Almost every night, those who worked in the machine shop would take a break to eat some soft ice cream.

Said Kidder: "Those of us who remained on board worked all night every night repairing equipment for the Army. We continued to make the Canopus appear to be abandoned in hopes the Japanese bombers would leave us alone. During the day we left it and slept in the hills wherever we could find a flat, non-rocky place to lay down. I don't know of any Navy ships that came in during this period, but we didn't seem to run out of work." The ground forces, both American and Filipino, were now aware there was no hope of getting reinforcements or replacement military equipment, so they quickly turned to the Canopus to keep broken or battle-damaged pieces in operation.

✲ ✲ ✲

"Enlisted personnel usually are not privy to military information that the commanders receive," Kidder continued, "but it seemed to me that during January, February and most of March, 1942, there was a lull in the front-line fighting. We regularly saw soldiers from the front who brought equipment to be repaired, which indicates a lull, and the bombings of the area were quite a bit less frequent."

Richard Kidder's perception of a "lull" was correct. The U.S. Army's 50th anniversary analysis of Philippine fighting, which had access to records from the Japanese, had these things to say: "(Japan's) Imperial General Headquarters assigned Lt. Gen. Masaharu Homma, commander of the 14th Army, the task of conquering the Philippines. ... It gave General Homma an exact timetable: conquer Luzon in 50 days. After that, half of his forces would be removed for operations scheduled elsewhere in Southeast Asia." By January 6, 1942, the Japanese had suffered 7,000 battle casualties, with another 10,000 or more inflicted with tropical diseases that had not been anticipated ... the same diseases affecting the Allied troops on Bataan.

There were other reasons for the delay in the final push against Bataan. The *American Heritage* summary of Japanese strategy noted that as soon as one island or nation was secured, at least half of the Japanese troops would be pulled out and moved immediately to the next target. Thus, when Manila fell early in January, the Japanese Imperial Army headquarters assumed General Homma was meeting his timetable, for they transferred the experienced 48th division, General Homma's best troops, to invade the Dutch East Indies.

Thus, there was a lull, caused by the unexpected tenacity of American and Filipino opposition as they backed into, and dug in, on Bataan; jungle diseases they were unprepared for; and Japanese Imperial Army mistakes that took away some of their best troops at a crucial time. Unable to break through American and Filipino lines on Bataan with the forces at hand, General Homma was forced to call on Imperial headquarters for reinforcements before renewing the final battle to secure the Philippines.

It was during the lull in fighting on Bataan that the Canopus' Executive Officer, Commander Goodall, summoned Kidder and another first class metalsmith, Ed Hall, into his office one evening and asked if they would consider being recommended for promotion to Warrant Officer-Carpenter. Among Warrant and Chief Warrant officers are the specialized, skilled personnel in specific fields such as repair, engineering, radio, electronics, etc., who rank between enlisted personnel and commissioned officers. Actually, they are commissioned officers but rank just below an ensign. It seems the Navy Department, obviously wanting to retain all of the skilled people possible, had notified commanding officers of ships to recommend those first class and chief petty officers that they felt were qualified, for promotion to Warrant officer. The exec told them to go out on deck and discuss it.

Here is how Kidder remembers it: "Ed Hall was three or four years older than I was, and much more mature. He had also been in the Navy longer than I. He had a wife and children back in the States. He told me flatly that there would be only two things which could happen to us – we would either be killed or we would be taken prisoner. In either case, Ed Hall felt, his family would receive much better financial compensation if he were an officer. I was only 23 years old and single. Obviously I didn't want to die, and I was as scared as anybody during bombings, but I hadn't given any consideration to the long range effect of the plight we were in. At any rate we went back in the office and answered in the affirmative; we would accept the commissions." Both commissions as Warrant Officers were approved, dated in June, 1942, but Richard Kidder would not know that until after the war was over.

Although skirmishes continued in the hills, the lull in aggressive fighting on Bataan, which lasted from early January to mid-March, also gave some much needed rest to most of the American and Filipino troops, but survival and living conditions became progressively worse.

John R. Bumgarner was a young Army doctor in General Hospital #2 on Bataan. In his 1995 book *Parade of the Dead* he described the medical situation on that rugged peninsula this way: "War plan Orange called for an armed force of about 30,000 men to retreat to Bataan. ...In actuality, about 80,000 troops and 26,000 civilians were on the peninsula (including the crew of the Canopus)." All told, Dr. Bumgarner said, there were " ... 120,000 miserable, starved, malaria-infected persons who were trapped like animals."

General MacArthur had ordered Bataan on half rations (less than 2,000 calories a day) in January. As time went by, this was reduced until – at the end – everyone was on one-fourth rations. By early March, Dr. Bumgarner noted, "...after prolonged dependence on a diet lacking the entire B spectrum, almost every patient showed some signs of deficiency diseases."

And it wasn't just food. They had run low on medications very early on, and were totally out of some. "By late February," Dr. Bumgarner said, "some units in the combat area had a 70 to 80 percent incidence of malarial infections." During the entire campaign, he estimated, "malaria and other tropical diseases were to take more casualties than the Japanese."

✳ ✳ ✳

In March the Japanese Philippine command received replacements to fill out the 16th division and the 65th brigade, in addition to units of Japan's 4th division, just arrived from China. The heavy fighting on Bataan renewed in late March, and the expected Japanese attack finally began on April 3rd after a sustained aerial and artillery bombardment.

"The big guns were booming day and night and bombing occurred constantly," Richard Kidder recalls. The fighting raged, and as it became clear that the American forces could no longer hold the Japanese at bay, the crew of the Canopus made its move to go to Corregidor. On the night of April 9, 1942, Kidder and his shipmates spent the night destroying all the large machinery such as lathes, milling machines, torpedo repair equipment, etc., mostly using acetylene torches, so no equipment would be usable even if the Japanese were able to salvage the ship.

Early the next morning a small crew backed the Canopus out to deep water and did one of the most dreaded things a sailor can do: they scuttled their ship and watched it sink into the deep waters of Manila Bay.

The Roscoe book on submarine operations says: "…Canopus remained with her submariners to go down in history as the indomitable 'Old Lady', supporting not only the hard-driven submarines but also the embattled defenders who fought to the last at Bataan."

The Canopus crew went by boat to Corrregidor. On April 10, 1942 the American forces on Bataan surrendered, and the only significant military barrier between Japan and Port Moresby, near Australia, was the rock fortress at the entrance of Manila Harbor named Corregidor.

✳ ✳ ✳

The surrender of American and Filipino troops on Bataan marks one of the most devastating losses ever incurred by an American military force. The horrors and brutality of the Japanese as they herded debilitated American prisoners along on the infamous "Bataan Death March" was merely a prelude to other atrocities committed by the troops from the land of the rising sun. But those now holding out on Corregidor had no time to consider that. They had problems of their own.

The USS Canopus, built in 1919 as a merchant ship, was acquired from the Grace Line in 1921 and converted to become a submarine tender. It was refitted with forges, machine shops, welding and other equipment needed to maintain and repair submarines and other military equipment. Known as the "Indomitable Old Lady" of the Pacific submarine force, she was named Canopus for the third brightest star in the universe. This photograph was acquired from the United States Naval Institute.

Chapter 5

FIGHTING THE JAPANESE —

THE 27 DAYS ON CORREGIDOR

Those who had been working to destroy the equipment on the Canopus got in small boats before dawn on April 10, 1942 and headed out for Corregidor Island, about three miles away. "It was about daylight when we arrived, and we found the rest of the Canopus crew," Kidder remembers. "They had set up a small camp with a field kitchen and we were fed breakfast. It was a hot cereal, a lot like oatmeal but they told us it was made of 'cracked wheat.' It wasn't bad considering the circumstances. They must have had a good bit of this 'cracked wheat' for we had it as bread later on." No one seemed to know where the cracked wheat came from, but it was welcome and certainly a lot better than rice.

"After we ate, we were told to take our sea bags and our hammock and head out across the island to a place called James Ravine." Kidder remembers. "On the map Corregidor looks like a pretty flat island, but believe me, it is not. A sea bag is heavy, the trail was steep and rocky, the Philippine sun was hot, and most in our small group had had very little sleep. Oh, and I was carrying a shotgun, but that is another story." There was one flat area along the way, a section of the island called "Middleside." This was where enlisted Army personnel were housed before the bombing began, and although it was a flat area that made walking easier, it had been heavily bombed and shelled and was covered with debris. Every so often the group was subjected to Japanese shelling from Bataan, and then Japanese planes would swoop over dropping bombs. It was obvious a major battle was underway, and the crew of the Canopus was right in the middle of it.

Kidder remembers very well one incident along the trail. "As I left the coast where we had landed and slowly trudged up the steep mountain," Kidder says, "I passed my friend, Ed Hall, sitting on the side of the road, resting. The road had been cut out of a steep hillside, and it was rocky. Ed was sitting on the ground, leaning back against the hill. We asked him to join us, but he said there was no hurry. He would be along later, he said. I'm usually a stickler for following orders, and I guess this was one of those times because I kept moving." It took most of the day but eventually the small group arrived at James Ravine. They were all exhausted.

The next chapter of this story is disheartening, but let Richard Kidder tell it as he remembers it: "When I lined up to get my supper someone came up to me and told me that I was to report immediately to Malinta Tunnel … the Navy Tunnel within Malinta. I was hot and tired, and didn't want to retrace a goodly portion of the trek I had just finished. I couldn't imagine what someone would want with me immediately. And anyway, the bombing might stop at dark, but the shelling was still going on and I would have to go back through that. So I told the guy that gave me the message that I would report to the Malinta Tunnel first thing in the morning. That's what I did, and I found out it was too late. The day before, a submarine lay at the bottom of the bay adjacent to the Malinta Tunnel. After nightfall that evening it surfaced and took on stores and personnel. They had searched for all of the 25 or so first class and chiefs who had been recommended for Warrant Officer rank, and those they found were loaded on board and by midnight the submarine and its passengers were on their way to Australia. Ed Hall was among them."

"I do not know of any single decision I have made in my entire life that had such a profound effect on my future," Kidder said later. "I ran into Ed Hall at the Naval Station, San Diego (several years later) and we shared some of our experiences. I learned first hand what one bad decision could make on one's life."

The James Ravine road was cut along the side of the mountain, similar to all mountain roads, so it was not easy for the sailors and the other troops assigned to this area to find a flat spot to sleep. "But digging a foxhole quickly became our number one priority," Kidder says. "We had hardly arrived when the shelling and bombing picked up. It was hard, rocky soil and the digging was hard. We would get tired and quit digging to rest, but the minute a few bombs dropped in our area we would get back at the digging, pronto. One has to be there, I suppose, to understand the intimidating feeling of that deafening sound when a bomb goes off nearby, or the feel of the whole earth vibrating under you. A couple of shipmates and I went some little distance below the road and dug our foxholes in the side of the mountain. The land was so steep it was more like digging a small cave than a foxhole. The other two fellows slept in their foxhole, but I slept right outside mine and rolled into it when a few bombs dropped near us."

"I don't know how many of us were killed while we were at James Ravine, but I know a number were. I can remember only one specific death, a first class metalsmith named Kennedy who was from Arkansas. He had dug a long, slender foxhole alongside the road, about knee deep, and he would lie in this during shelling and air raids. But on this particular raid some other sailor had beat him to his trench. He ran the man out of his foxhole and lay face down in it, covering his head. A bomb burst fairly close by, and a stray piece of shrapnel entered his foxhole and cut his spine in half. Fate is a funny thing."

James Ravine was on the side of Corregidor closest to Bataan, an easy target for the Japanese artillery, and a major gun emplacement was just uphill from the area assigned to the Canopus sailors. The Japanese would often use that gun emplacement as their target, and the exploding shells would send an avalanche of rock and concrete tumbling down through James Ravine. Eventually, a Japanese shell got to the ammunition magazine and there was a huge explosion, killing several GI's in the area and sending a mass of rock fragments thundering through the area where Richard Kidder had dug his foxhole. In this case he and his nearby foxhole neighbors were not hurt. Fate is, indeed, a funny thing.

A Marine lieutenant was assigned the duty of taking the "rag-tag" sailors on Corregidor, and shaping them into an infantry fighting unit … some even called it the Navy Battalion. When Kidder left the Canopus he brought a 12 gauge shotgun and some shells with him. "I never could shoot," he said. "Growing up I couldn't hit the side of a barn with a rifle. I figured if I had to shoot somebody I would come nearer doing it with a shotgun than a rifle." The Marine lieutenant would have no part of it. He made Kidder swap his shotgun for a rifle, telling him "this is not an exercise where you wait till you see the whites of their eyes before you shoot." Then the Marine added a postscript: "but you do wait long enough to be sure you are shooting the enemy. I don't want you shooting one of our own people, you know." Where they came from is still a mystery, but the sailors were given boxes of World War I Enfield rifles and told to unpack them. Kidder remembers "…they were wrapped in cosmoline and old newspapers, with dates on the newspapers of about 1920, or maybe even earlier." There was ammunition for the old rifles, too.

Richard Kidder "celebrated" – if you can call it that – his 24th birthday on May 4, 1942, hunkered down in a foxhole on Corregidor, with plenty of fireworks, waiting for the inevitable. A U.S. Army postwar analysis of the Corregidor defense stated that on that May 4 enemy shells were falling at the rate of every five seconds. In the 24 hours of Richard Kidder's birthday 16,000 Japanese shells exploded on the small island of Corregidor. And that did not take into account the bombs that fell. It was obvious the Japanese were "softening up" the American troops for their long-delayed invasion.

Then early on the morning of May 6 this Navy land-fighting unit was "awakened", and began its march to face the invading Japanese soldiers on the other end of the island. The Navy unit marched through the Malinta tunnel and downhill toward the long curving, flat, sandy tail of the island. The Japanese troops were literally landing by the thousands at a beach called Monkey Point. The only other things out there were a lot of sand, a radio tower and a landing strip. The Navy unit marched past the North dock, on their left, and the South dock, on their right, both by now piles of rubble, and onto a barren coastal area. "I don't remember any well defined front line, such as trenches, for instance," Kidder said. "We just walked up to where the firing of rifles from both sides demanded that we halt. I don't remember actually seeing a Japanese soldier, but we knew they were there because bullets were flying all over the place. I had been taught not to fire unless you knew what you were shooting at, lest you shoot one of your own. I was aware Americans were being shot on either side of me." Kidder remembers the noise was immense. And constant. A thundering roar.

For Richard Kidder and the other members of the "Navy Battalion", the melee as they faced the Japanese was a chaotic blur. To this day they have a hard time describing it. Researching other sources we find these thoughts and memories: "If Hollywood had done a movie depicting the end of the world, it would have looked just like Corregidor the day the Japanese landed there." The sound "hurt your ears." Explosions. Fiery balls and huge booms. The ground you were standing on vibrated. Machine guns and rifles were the least of the noise. "There was this haze covering everything, and the acrid smell of gunpowder."

Records show the Japanese landed several thousand men, and some 6,000 were killed. Casualties were unimportant to the Japanese high command, and death was an honor to the Japanese soldier. A unit of American Marines had met the Japanese landing party first, and held them momentarily. But the Japanese troops just kept coming, and now they were breaking through and over-running the makeshift units, including the "Navy Battalion."

"In the midst of all this I heard my name being called," Kidder remembers. "It was a Navy Lieutenant off the Canopus, and next to him was a Navy Machinists Mate who had just had most of his left arm shot off. The Lieutenant ordered me to put a tourniquet on the man's arm and get him back to the hospital in the tunnel, and do it quickly. Then the lieutenant turned back to being a rifleman, just like the rest of us."

"I have no idea how far we were from the entrance to the Melinta Tunnel, or how long it took us to get there. I know it was a struggle, and it couldn't have taken too long or he would have bled to death. I remember we came into the open and Japanese planes were flying all over the place, but they did not strafe us. As we crossed the barren area I remember seeing another American walking toward the tunnel. I called to him and asked him to help me, but he said he, too, was wounded. It seemed like it took me forever to get this man to the hospital, but probably not. Anyway, I turned my patient over to an Army nurse, who promptly ran me out of the hospital."

Kidder continues: "In the quiet of the tunnel it suddenly hit me that we hadn't had anything to eat that day. I was hungry and very, very thirsty. I finally found some coffee and something to eat … I don't remember what … and I think I would have liked to linger a while, but my conscience wouldn't let me, so I finally started my reluctant way back to the front." And then, gradually, all the noise stopped. And it got ghostly quiet.

"Before I made it back to my unit, the fighting was over." Kidder recalls. "General Wainwright had surrendered all of the Philippines. I think this was about 11 to 12 a.m. on May 6, 1942."

For Richard Kidder, his days of combat were over. His "grand finale" as an American fighting man had not come aboard a Navy ship, but as a rifleman and a medic facing a suicidal charge by Japanese land troops. And now the ordeal of becoming a Japanese prisoner of war was to begin.

✲ ✲ ✲

It had been 27 days since Richard Kidder left Bataan and became a part of the defense force on Corregidor. Some military historians say those 27 days changed the direction of World War II in the Pacific.

The United States Army's 50th Anniversary of Victory study of the Philippines Islands Campaign had these things to say:

> "For all the courage and resourcefulness of the Philippine defenders, their fate was sealed when the Japanese crippled the U.S. Pacific Fleet at Pearl Harbor on December 7, 1941, and virtually destroyed U.S. air power in the Philippines a few hours later. Without the fleet or covering air units, it was only a matter of time. Cut off from all support and heavily outnumbered by a determined enemy, the American and Filipino units faced annihilation or surrender."
>
> "The valiant defense of the Philippines had several important consequences. It delayed the Japanese timetable for the conquest of south Asia, causing them to expend far more manpower and materiel resources than anticipated. Probably of equal importance, the determined resistance against overwhelming odds

became a symbol of hope for the United States in the early, bleak days of the war."

And some insist the extra 27 days that America held out on Corregidor, after Bataan fell, helped give the United States Navy the time necessary to reassemble its fleet and meet the Japanese Navy head on in the Battle of the Coral Sea, stopping cold the Japanese uninterrupted march through the South Pacific. And only a month later, the U.S. Navy decisively defeated the Japanese Navy in the Battle of Midway ... the naval battle recognized by most historians as the turning point of World War II in the Pacific.

The World War II memorial in Washington, D. C., has carved in stone this tribute to the men who fought in the Battle of Midway: "They had no right to win, yet they did, and in so doing they changed the course of a war ... even against the greatest of odds, there is something in the human spirit – a magic blend of skill, faith and valor – that can lift men from certain defeat to incredible victory." The words are those of author Walter Lord, and they could apply to every man who, hanging on against the greatest of odds at Bataan and Corregidor, slowed the Japanese onslaught and thus helped make the incredible victory possible at the Battle of Midway.

Chapter 6

AMERICA'S RALLYING CRY:

REMEMBER PEARL HARBOR

Back home in America there was frantic activity. The bombing of Pearl Harbor had totally quieted the caustic political debate between isolationists and interventionists ... those Americans who wanted to stay out of the war no matter what, and those who felt the United States should intervene and get involved, even if it was only to provide supplies and equipment to the Allies. Very few government leaders proposed going to war before December 7, 1941. A united, and now patriotic, America had emerged from the ashes of December 7, and the battle cry of all America was "Remember Pearl Harbor." Men were enlisting for combat duty; women were volunteering for non-combat duty; young men were being drafted into the armed forces. Labor's work week was extended, and a War Production Board was harnessing America's manufacturing might to produce war goods (between July 31, 1941, and July 1, 1945, America's manufacturing plants turned out 296,601 aircraft; 71,060 ships; and 86,388 tanks).

Despite the patriotic fervor, the early days of World War II marked a very disturbing, almost desperate time for the people of the United States. The military news out of Europe and North Africa was not good. There was daily news of ships being sunk by German U-boats in the Atlantic …some of them American, and some in sight of our coastline. The string of Japanese victories in the Pacific was unbroken.

David Boyle's *History of World War II* describes this point in time this way: "… within three months, Japan had broken the American blockade, taken control of the Dutch oilfields and cowed the British Empire. It also now controlled all of the world's rubber and 70 percent of the world's tin. The 'Co-prosperity sphere' was complete. It was an extra-ordinary achievement (by the Japanese)."

Back home, it was a bleak time indeed, and yet America had a great and determined spirit.

✫ ✫ ✫

The one bright spot during this era was the courageous defense being put up by American and Filipino troops on Luzon, in the Philippines. The American GI's on Bataan and Corregidor became the heart of their nation … the proof positive that this country would stand and fight. William Manchester, in his biography of General Douglas McArthur, said: "The gallant defense of Bataan (and Corregidor), and General McArthur's dramatic communiques, were capturing the imagination of the country. … U.S. eyes were riveted on the Philippines."

Americans were told by the media that every day the hard pressed, but superbly brave, American troops held out on Bataan and Corregidor, the greater our chance to reassemble naval and air power in the Pacific. And yet, there was great concern about what would happen to our troops if they should fall into the hands of the Japanese.

During their conquest of China in the 1930's, the Japanese had earned a reputation for brutality toward any enemy, and especially prisoners of war. Their warrior culture demanded that their own soldiers should fight to the death. To surrender was cowardly, and in Japanese culture cowards lost face. David Boyle, in the chapter of his book on World War II entitled *Japanese Atrocities: The Crimes of The Empire of the Sun* noted: "According to the Japanese military code of *bushido*, prisoners had surrendered all honour along with their freedom, and with honour had gone the right to humane consideration. ... For the 'dishonour' of not fighting to the death, Western POWs were regularly beaten, starved, denied medical treatment, subjected to bizarre medical experiments or worked to death. No one was spared."

Japan had refused to become a signatory to the Geneva Conventions, the world treaty on the treatment of prisoners of war. The Japanese warrior could have respect for an enemy who fought to the death, but had the attitude that an enemy who surrendered deserved to die. They also felt it fair to intimidate their foe through brutal treatment of an enemy soldier, the soldier's family, or anyone else who would weaken the fighting spirit of their enemy.

This was a hard lesson for Americans to learn and accept as they fought face-to-face with Japanese soldiers in the islands of the South Pacific. One in three of all Americans captured by the Japanese in World War II died while a prisoner, and the death rate was even higher in the early days of the war. By comparison, less than two percent of American POWs in German prison camps died.

✻ ✻ ✻

The news of Bataan's capitulation saddened all America, but the later news of the Bataan Death March was even more devastating. Said the *American Heritage* report of this news: "The story shocked and enraged America and hardened its resolution to defeat Japan."

April 9, 1942, was the day Bataan was surrendered, and the Japanese immediately started the debilitated American and Filipino survivors on a 65-mile forced march to a former military encampment called Camp O'Donnell. These prisoners were spurred along in the broiling sun with little or no water, no food, no rest, clubbed and prodded with bayonets, and when they fell, they were often shot on the spot or their heads lopped off with the famed razor-sharp Japanese sword. It was estimated that 7,000 to 10,000 American and Filipino soldiers perished on the Bataan Death March. The news of the deliberate and arbitrary cruelty by the Japanese, against Americans on the death march came out bit by bit in America, sickening and angering the people "back home". But the worst was yet to come. Of the 54,000 who made it to Camp O'Donnel, 40 percent would die of malnutrition, disease and sickness, or torture and cruelty from sadistic guards.

It was 27 days after the surrender of Bataan, May 6, 1942, that Corregidor finally fell. During this time the military communications people in the Malinta Tunnel on Corregidor had been listening to various news reports on short-wave radio, just as General McArthur had before he left for Australia. Said

Richard Kidder: "We all had heard war stories about how the Japanese treated their prisoners, and we had heard rumors about the death march from Bataan." Thus the news about brutal treatment by the Japanese was no surprise. It was what they expected.

One observer of the news in America summed it up this way: General McArthur's defense of the Philippines "was the one creditable episode of the whole first five months of the war in the Pacific." It stood out, George Kenney said, "…like a beacon of hope in comparison with the incredible debacle at Singapore, the easy fall of the Dutch East Indies, and the confusion in Washington."

But most devastating of all, for the families back home who had loved ones in the Philippines, such as Richard Kidder's, was the total lack of news about individual American servicemen. There was the gnawing fear that came from simply not knowing the fate of their loved ones. Red Cross inspectors were not allowed by the Japanese to visit in Japanese "war zones." They were not allowed to gather POW names. Neither were they allowed to transmit letters to or from Japanese prisoners. David Boyle reported that "the first full reports of the Bataan Death March did not emerge until Spring,1943, and even then the true facts were held back (by the Allies) for fear they would affect civilian morale."

It would be a full year before Richard Kidder's mother was notified that he was officially "missing in action." And it would be two years before she received a report from the American military, transmitted through the Red Cross, that there was a

Navy man named Richard Kidder listed as a "prisoner of war" in Japan.

But Richard Kidder, once he became a prisoner of the Japanese, knew even less about news from America, and more to the point, he knew nothing at all about the progress of America's war with Japan. The last he knew was that the Japanese seemed invincible in the Pacific; that the Germans appeared to be winning in Europe; that the Philippines were now in Japanese hands; and that he was a prisoner of war.

Chapter 7

PRISONER OF WAR – THE PHILIPPINES

It was about noontime on May 6, 1942, that things began to get quiet on Corregidor. There is uncertainty just how the word spread down through the ranks to both the Japanese and Americans on the front lines that General Wainwright had surrendered the American forces to Japan. At about 11 a.m. bullets were flying: soldiers on both sides were forcing their way forward or falling, and the noise was immense and continuous. Some military historians have called it a perfect example of "the fog of war" on the front lines. Then, little by little the shooting dropped off until there was an eerie silence. And, no doubt, there was this thought all along the front: now what?

For Richard Kidder, the next few hours remain a chaotic blur. He is not sure how he got back from the hospital in the Melinta Tunnel to his unit, but he must have, for the next thing he remembers clearly is when he and his shipmates from the Canopus were being herded by threatening Japanese soldiers onto an open area, a beach, along with other American prisoners. (It is likely that as many as 3,000 to 5,000 American GI's – Marines, soldiers, sailors – were gathered together on this remote beach, around a small cove, somewhere between Melinta Mountain and Monkey Point).

These American GI's had held out for 27 more days after Bataan fell (during which the Bataan Death March took place). Those left had lived through constant artillery shelling, incessant bombing, limited sleep in rocky foxholes, partial rations, and now they were weary, physically drained, and at the same time anxious. Not all came out of this ordeal alive. After the war was over, a monument was erected on Corregidor that says:

Sleep my sons, your duty done …
For freedom's light has come.
Sleep in the silent depths of the sea
Or in your bed of hallowed sod.
Until you hear at dawn
The low clear reveille of God.

The poet is unknown, but it is said that the monument is designed so that each May 6, at 12 noon, the sun is in such a position that its rays fall precisely into the monument's center. It is a remembrance of the Pacific War Dead.

For Richard Kidder and the other Americans, day followed day in which they just sat there on the beach, in the blistering Philippine sun. There was no shade. One prisoner put it this way: "The thermometer was stuck at 95 degrees." No food was issued the Americans during this period. The troops suffered more from a lack of drinking water, however, than from lack of food. Said Kidder: "Every so often small details of prisoners were formed to trudge over to the (Melinta) mountain to bring back as many canteens of water as they could carry. Somewhere on Melinta Mountain there was a water spigot where we filled our canteens. But these water details had to be guarded by a Japanese soldier so the details were small and far between. I only remember making the trip once. The extremely hot seashore sun and the lack of water really took its toll on us."

To make matters worse, there were no toilet facilities. "The only solution was for the horde of us to use the small bay as our toilet. It was a secluded bay so whatever floated in it stayed in it, and didn't wash out to sea. Our beach quickly became a filthy, stinking mess."

Kidder has no idea how long the American prisoners were held there, but post-war writings from Japanese records indicate most of the Japanese soldiers were quickly moved to secure the southern Philippine islands, and the American prisoners on Corregidor were simply held there until some Japanese troops could be sent back, while other Japanese were sent to new battle fronts. It is likely the Americans received four weeks of what became known as "the Japanese sun treatment for prisoners" in the sun-baked tropical islands of the South Pacific. The Americans were always "dry-mouth thirsty". Some died, and the others were weak, weary, dirty and unshaven with tattered and filthy uniforms. (Manila is at about the same latitude as the Caribbean, south of Cuba, with a tropical climate).

Eventually the Japanese military turned attention back to the prisoners on Corregidor, and started loading them into small boats. They were taken across the bay in the general direction of Manila, but were landed several miles north of town, at the end of a beautiful and spacious road called Dewey Boulevard (no doubt named for the American Admiral Dewey). It soon became apparent that this was to be a Japanese Victory March, a strategy to intimidate the Philippine population, and to impress the Filipinos with the might of the Japanese Army. Says Kidder: "They had us march in a very round-about way through much of Manila. It was a victory march for them; they wanted the Philippine citizens to see what a sorry lot the American soldiers and sailors had become. And we were a sorry lot. They marched us through town to an old Spanish-American War prison called Bilibid."

Kidder spent only one night in Bilibid; the next day they loaded him on a railroad boxcar. Richard Gordon, in his *Bataan, Corregidor and the Death March: In Retrospect* indicates that generally "…the prisoners were forced into 1918 model railroad boxcars (40X8) used in France during World War I. With over 100 men squeezed into each car, the Japanese then forced the doors closed. There was no room to sit down or fall down. Men died in the sweltering cars." Kidder's group was shipped about 100 miles north of Manila to a town named Cabanatuan.

There were three camps for prisoners of war in the Cabanatuan area. Cabanatuan #1 became famous for its brutal treatment of prisoners, and for the number who died there. It also gained notoriety late in the war when a group of American Rangers stormed through hostile territory and released the Americans still alive there. #1 was in the edge of Cabanatuan. Cabanatuan #2 had no water, and the Japanese eventually ceased using it. Then there was Cabanatuan #3 which was located about six miles out of town.

In the luck of the draw, Richard Kidder's group of American prisoners was force-marched from the railroad station in town to Cabanatuan #3. They had no idea they had drawn the "best" camp at the time, though, for they were forced to trudge on to their new quarters instead of stopping off at Cabanatuan #1. Said Kidder: "I was part of the large group (of prisoners) who were marched, herded would be a better description, to Camp #3." This Camp #3 had been a Philippine Army Camp, and by after-the-war comparison with other Japanese prison camps it was fairly acceptable. "The barracks were made of bamboo and were reasonably comfortable and airy. We had no bedding, of course, but the wooden platforms we slept on were covered with straw matting. There was a water spigot handy so we had drinking water and every once in a while we were even permitted to bathe in the small river that ran through camp."

"However, having your friends die around you, especially when there is nothing you can do about it, and when there seems to be no light at the end of the tunnel, takes its toll."

"It was while we were in this prison camp that one of my very best friends, Blackie, an old World War I blacksmith, died of a heart attack. He had taught me the rudiments of machine blacksmithing. He had been like a father to me. I was one of his friends who helped dig his grave, place his naked body in it, and then cover it with dirt. That was hard to do." But, at least, that was a natural death.

The Japanese also used terroristic executions to keep people in line; not only prisoners of war, but their own people, too. "I have been asked why more of us didn't try to escape," Kidder says. "Some in Germany did. The primary reason was that an American in the Philippines or in Japan would stick out like a sore thumb. Unless you had a very good native friend who would hide you and forage for your food, there was no way you could go undetected. And the natives learned very quickly that if they did such a thing, not only would they be executed but their whole family would, too."

"The other reason was that we learned very quickly that even to try such a thing would bring on torture and execution. To give you an example: Four young American soldiers did escape while we were being marched from town to camp #3. They were captured within 12 hours. They were made to kneel with a stick under their knees ... it causes excruciating pain, try it sometime ... in front of the Japanese commander's office while a court martial was being held. Early the next morning they were taken to four newly dug graves where they were shot. Right out in the open in a part of the camp where everybody could see it. I was on the other side of the camp, and I refused to watch the execution, but all of us heard the shots and knew what had happened. Some might still have tried to escape, but we all knew the odds of passing as natives was nil, and we had been shown the savage nature of Japanese justice if we tried it."

Later, the Japanese initiated another system to discourage escapes. Each prisoner was assigned to a group of 10, referred to (by the prisoners) as "Blood Brothers." If one member of that group escaped, or even attempted to escape, all 10 would be immediately shot.

Other vague things also let the prisoners know that life in this prisoner of war camp would have its sordid moments. During the rainy season, the Cabanatuan prison camps were an ooze of sticky mud, and in the dry season, powdery dust. "Lack of food began to take its toll," Kidder remembers. "Many of us developed beri-beri and night blindness. Our toilets were the famous army style slit trenches about six feet deep. These open pits attracted flies in droves. I have never seen so many large green flies in my life. They were everywhere and on everything. Except for these flies, very little food, and sheer boredom, this camp (compared to others) could not be considered a bad one. We were neither harassed nor bothered." During this time, Kidder developed yellow jaundice and malaria. "I didn't mind the jaundice so much because I had very little food anyway, but the malaria was pure hell with no medicine."

Dr. John R. Bumgarner was in Cabanatuan #1 which was still losing 20 to 30 prisoners a day, but the disease problems he encountered were prevalent in Cabanatuan #3 as well. Dr. Bumgarner recalled that some prisoners simply died of starvation, and that dry beri-beri was "the most resistant to treatment of all our problems." Among other problems reported by Dr. Bumgarner …

… malaria, which could have been controlled with quinine. Without medication it caused chills, headaches and high fever.

… blindness, due to vitamin B-1 deficiency.

… dysentery, both amoebic and bacillary.

… diarrhea.

… the lice and bedbug problem remained, and the area was never free of mosquitos. In the rainy season "the ants came in." Then there were always the swarms of large green flies. There was a general lack of sanitation, the doctor recalled, and the open pit toilets formed a fertile breeding ground for the flies.

… there were other problems, like pellagra, skin infections and in layman's terms, yellow jaundice. And GIs throughout the Pacific theater of war suffered from the fungus problem generally referred to as "jungle rot".

It was hot during the rainy season, and the high humidity intensified many problems. "The diet was just sufficient in quality (and quantity) to keep many just barely hanging on", noted Dr. Bumgarner. "For me as a doctor, the most distressing thought was that they could have been saved, almost without exception, by proper diet and medical care."

It wasn't only the American military prisoners who received this type mis-treatment; American civilians who were trapped in the Philippines did also. In a special report in U.S. News & World Report, dated as late as July, 2006, it was noted an American Red Cross worker named Marie Adams had written about her experience while interned by the Japanese in a Manila camp for more than three years. Said Adams: "When we read that each week a food kit was being distributed to prisoners held in Europe, I think our morale hit an all-time low. We had known that we were isolated from the world, but the fact was truly driven home to us by that information more than anything else. We felt that we were indeed the 'lost tribes of the Philippines' – no contact with home, no contact with the Red Cross, no contact with the outside at all, and none to be expected." She went on to say: "we were hungry; we were starved." She weighed 95 pounds when liberated.

Richard Kidder spent the summer of 1942 at Cabanatuan #3 in the Philippines, "just laying around and wasting away."

The last news these prisoners had received of the war against Japan was, if you were an American, bad news. And what little scuttlebutt they picked up in their secluded prison environment was even worse. Of the Americans who were captured on Bataan, and went on the infamous Death March and into O'Donnell or Cabanatuan #1, two out of every three did not live to return home after the war. Many on the Death March were stabbed to death with a bayonet, or had their heads lopped off with the single swing of a Japanese sword ... always where other prisoners could see the event. Others died in the prison. By comparison "only" one out of every three from Corregidor lost his life while traveling to, and existing, in Cabanatuan #3.

But, back home, there was some encouraging news. On 18 April 1942 Jimmy Doolittle's famed raiders boldly flew B-25 bombers from the mystical "Shangri-La" and bombed Tokyo. Then 4–8 May 1942 the Americans stymied the Japanese movement toward Australia in the first great naval battle of World War II, the Battle of the Coral Sea. And on 3–6 June 1942, the United States Navy won a stunning victory over the Japanese fleet in the Battle of Midway. It was not known at the time, of course, but the Battle of Midway is generally considered the turning point of the war in the pacific.

There was no way for these prisoners of war to know the good news from the rest of the world, and there was no way for them to understand that their life at Cabanatuan #3 was pretty good compared with the brutal treatment many American prisoners of war were receiving in other prison camps.

But for Richard Kidder, the "good" treatment was about to end.

Chapter 8

LIFE AND DEATH ON A JAPANESE *HELL SHIP*

Richard Kidder had been a prisoner of war for about six months in the Philippines when, in the fall of 1942, a large group of American prisoners were yanked from Cabanatuan to go to Japan. He was a little guy, able to get by on the sparse rations better than some of his fellow prisoners, and at this point appeared reasonably healthy. It is likely the Japanese chose prisoners who appeared to be physically fit and capable of heavy manual labor, for that was what they would end up doing on the Japanese homeland. The chosen POWs were again stuffed in railroad boxcars in the searing Philippine heat to be transported to Manila. No one sat down, or even fell down; they were packed too tightly for that.

Kidder remembers the trip from Manila to Japan as a living nightmare, the most dreadful episode in his entire three-and-a-half year experience as a prisoner of the Japanese.

It was about October 15, 1942, when the American prisoners were crammed into the extreme bottom hold of a small Japanese freighter. It was steamy hot, and there was no fresh air except the minute amount that leaked through the small hatch in the top of the hold. Japanese soldiers were on the deck above them. "I don't know how many of us were packed into this small space," Kidder recalls, "but there were at least three times too many." The hold had been fitted with double-deck platforms, supposedly to be used as bunks, but there were so many prisoners that all of them could not sit or lie down at the same time. Most of the American prisoners teamed up with a buddy to swap resting periods.

There were no toilet facilities. The Japanese soldiers above them went to a rigged "out-house" hung out over the stern of the ship, but the American prisoners were not allowed to go topside. A couple of large wooden buckets were lowered into the center of the prisoner's quarters for everyone to use. Said Kidder: "It seemed they were full all the time. The Japanese were not in a hurry to hoist them topside for emptying. Try to picture hundreds of us cooped up in this hot, almost airless hold and every time the ship rolled (which was constantly) they would slop over and spill out. We were a filthy lot." Since many of the prisoners had dysentery when they came aboard, the atmosphere was putrid from the very beginning.

It didn't take long for Richard Kidder to imagine that being dead would be better than life on this *Hell Ship*. His yellow jaundice completely destroyed any desire to take food, and every other day chills and fever from malaria turned severe. The prisoners were issued a very small amount of water once each day, and a small ration of rice. Kidder swapped his ration of rice to a shipmate for more time laying down.

Kidder was neither able to eat, nor did he have a bowel movement, during the entire trip to Japan. "I was so sick I didn't care about anything," he says. "It was the first time in my life that I simply wished I could die. I felt I would be better off. But I knew the conditions were just as bad for everyone else, maybe worse since I was able to lie down most of the time." He estimates they were on that ship four to six weeks. In the bottom of the ship it was neither day or night, so it was hard to keep track of time, even for those who were not sick. The convoy stopped one time, and the prisoners did learn that was in Formosa, but they were not allowed out of their prison in the dark, stuffy bottom hold of the ship. Post war records show stops like this were not unusual; they were likely waiting for the next convoy to form up before going back to sea.

Convoys traveled at the speed of the slowest ship. Richard Kidder had served on a submarine tender, and he knew American torpedoes could be very effective when an American submarine encountered a slow-moving convoy. He also knew the "whumph" sound of a depth charge, and that it likely meant a Japanese warship was stalking an Allied submarine, which in turn was stalking the convoy. Richard Kidder had great respect for the ability of American submariners.

At one time, Kidder's convoy was attacked by an American submarine, and the Japanese closed the hold and battened the hatches down tight. The POWs were locked in. Kidder still shudders at the terror the moment they learned what was going on. "If our ship was torpedoed, we would have gone down with it. I have read that, unfortunately, a goodly number of American prisoners did die this way. I changed my mind. I did not want to drown; certainly not that way. I decided I wanted to live, after all."

After the war it was confirmed that some ships carrying prisoners were torpedoed and sunk, and in some ships that were not sunk, some POWs went mad with thirst. One historian reported that "In December, 1944, over 1,600 maltreated Dutch, American and British prisoners were crammed below the decks of a ship to remove them from advancing American troops in the Philippines." That ship was torpedoed and sunk.

In due time, Kidder's *Hell Ship* docked in Yokohama, Japan, the blessed end of Richard Kidder's longest living nightmare. They had left Manila in mid-October, and as best they could calculate, back in America it was the day before Thanksgiving, 1942.

Filthy though they were, looking more like ghoulish ghosts than human beings, they were herded on a high-speed train to cover the 100 or so miles from Yokohama to Osaka. Then they were marched several blocks to a barn-like, three-story structure they called Umeda Bunsho. Umeda was a section of the city, they were to learn later, and they assumed Bunsho meant prison. Whatever the building was originally, it now was a POW barracks.

Inside, each of the three floors had long, wide "shelves" down each side of the long room, wide enough for two people to lie side by side. At least there was enough room in this POW facility for everyone to lie down. Down the middle of the room was a long table with wooden benches on each side. About the middle of the room was a hibachi-looking grill that certainly did not heat the room, although the prisoners were to learn later it did warm their hands when they returned from their day of labor.

The third floor was designated as the sick bay, and Richard Kidder was taken directly there the day he arrived. It was already winter in Japan, and the prisoners – coming from a warmer climate – were wearing summer clothes, some of them the military type short pants. Prisoners who were physically able were assigned immediately to work details.

Richard Kidder, deemed too weak to work, remained in sick bay. Rations included water and a very small ball of rice, usually a bit larger than a golf ball, but never as large as a baseball. Even though it was said there was one Army doctor available, there were no medications to treat them. The room was bitter cold.

"So we lay, side by side, waiting to die," Kidder recalls. "If you were sick and couldn't work because of dysentery or anything else, the Japanese had a unique system of healing. Normally we (Americans) give the sick richer food, but not them. The ration of rice given to all POWs was very meager, but when we couldn't work, our ration was cut in half. And to make matters worse, it was cooked similar to 'watery' oatmeal. You can imagine how much this helped those of us with dysentery."

"You guessed it," Kidder recalls. "We began dying like flies." More than 60 of the 250 to 300 American prisoners at Umeda Bunsho – mostly Navy and Marine personnel – died in the cold winter months of 1942–43. The Japanese simply hauled the dead out every morning. No one knew where they were taken.

The prisoners had not had a bath since leaving the Philippines, and all of them had a bad case of body lice. They could tell instantly when one of their number died, for the lice would leave the dead body and immediately migrate to the next person who was still alive.

For Richard Kidder days stretched into weeks, and weeks into months, lying on the cold shelves on the third floor of Umeda Bunsho. "In honesty I again wanted to die. I am sure that I would have eventually died," he recalls, "except I had a friend, Louie Nash, who came to see me after work each day to encourage me to get up, to fight for my life. He couldn't bring me food because he had none. He kept urging me to get up and go to work because he knew if I didn't I would shortly die."

"Finally," Kidder says, "he gave up on me and told me he wasn't coming to see me any more; if I didn't care about living, why should he. He literally goaded me into getting up off that sick bay floor and coming back to life. He made me so ashamed that the next day I volunteered to go to work. I was so weak I could hardly walk, but again God shined on me. I was assigned to the same small work detail that Louie worked on."

Although about one-fourth of the "healthy" prisoners brought in from the Philippines had now died, Richard Kidder had survived in the Umedo Bunsho sick bay from late November, 1942, to Spring, 1943 – about five months. Once on his feet, a miraculous recovery started. "I not only gained strength," he says, "but my body, with no medicine of any kind, healed itself. The warm weather, hard daily work, and a little more food cured my dysentery, yellow jaundice, malaria and whatever else I had, very effectively." He also believes he had one other thing going for him; he was smaller than most of the American prisoners. The larger-framed GIs got about the same amount of rice as the smaller ones. So long as they were physically healthy, they survived, even though their bodies became skin and bone. "But if they got sick for any reason," Kidder recalls, "they were goners."

Kidder figured he had lost down to about 90 pounds (because that is what he weighed when the war ended) but "it is amazing what a little more food, sunshine and hard daily labor did for my spirits. Not only was my body strengthened, but my mind was, too. I felt I could survive until the war was over, no matter how long that was."

Richard Kidder had now been a captive of the Japanese for one full year, and he had just fought off a deep desire to give in to his rotten circumstances and die. But having survived this long, he now adopted a fierce determination to live until this war was over, even though he had no idea what was happening in the war itself.

✲ ✲ ✲

A NOTE ABOUT THE *HELL SHIPS*

It was well after World War II ended that the scope of the *Hell Ship* story began to unfold. It was known that some Japanese ships with POWs aboard had been sunk, but these were apparently viewed as isolated events, not necessarily as part of a calculated Japanese war strategy. After the war, as families of lost or missing-in-action GIs sought information about the fate of their loved ones, the pattern of calculated forced-labor and brutality began to become apparent. Most early information about the *Hell Ships* came from isolated stories, such as the one included here from the experience of Richard Kidder, about GIs who had survived a *Hell Ship* trip, and especially from those few who had survived a trip in which their *Hell Ship* had been sunk.

A *Britain at War* report, from a study trying to find names of captured troops, said this: "After invading many countries in the Far East, Japan found themselves with a large amount of prisoners, but what to do with them? Japan decided to use them as slave labour to help their war effort, the majority being transported by ship to new destinations."

Ruth E. Jorgenson, in *The Hell Ships of World War II, described* them this way:

"Hell Ships were unmarked Japanese freighters used to transport American POWs during World War II. Because these ships were unmarked, Allied forces frequently targeted and torpedoed them. We had no way of knowing that our troops were packed like sardines in the holds of those freighters, with no chance of escape if the ship were hit. The result was that thousands of Allied troops lost their lives. America's finest young men, who had already endured many months of torture in disease-ridden POW camps without decent food or water, were being transported to Japan ... where they would work as slave laborers for the Japanese war effort."

A 2003 article in Prologue Magazine by Lee A. Gladwin (Archival Services Branch, Center for Electronic Records, National Archives and Records Administration) notes that much information about specific Japanese ships carrying POWs has been retrieved in recent years from wartime IBM punch cards. Gladwin also notes that Gregory Michno, in his book *Death on the Hellships: Prisoners at Sea in the Pacific War*, estimated that more than 126,000 Allied prisoners of war were transported in 156 voyages and that more than 21,000 Americans were killed or injured by attacks from American submarines or airplanes (the Americans not knowing POWs were aboard).

Possibly the most disheartening troop loss from the sinking of a single *Hell Ship* was the *Junyo Maru*, a cargo ship torpedoed off the western coast of Sumatra by a British submarine, the *HMS Tradewind*, in September, 1944. Of an estimated 6,500 prisoners from several Allied nations crammed into the hold, at least 5,640 went down with the ship.

Wikipedia reports on *Hell Ships* this way:

"As Allied forces closed in, the Japanese began transferring POWs by sea. Similar to conditions on the Bataan Death March, prisoners were often crammed into cargo holds with little air, food or water, for journeys that would last weeks. Many died due to asphyxia, starvation or dysentery. Some POWs in the heat, humidity, lack of oxygen, food and water became delirious.... Unlike weapons transports which were marked as Red Cross ships, these prisoner transports were unmarked and were targeted by Allied submarines, unaware of their real purpose."

The 2000 edition of the *Register of Graduates of the United States Military Academy* at West Point has a note concerning "WWII Deaths on Japanese Ships." The note states: "Beginning in 1944, there were a number of Allied attacks on Japanese ships that, unknown to the Allies, were evacuating prisoners of war to Japan." The Register gives some examples:

> 'POW ship 7 Sept. 44'. This was the Shinyo Maru torpedoed off Mindanao. Aboard were 750, of whom 82 survived, reached shore, and were rescued by guerillas."
> 'POW ship 24 Oct. 44'. This was the Arisan Maru, torpedoed about 200 miles off the Southeast China coast. Aboard were 1,790, of whom five reached shore and were rescued by the Chinese."
> 'POW ship15 Dec. 44'. This was the Oryoku Maru, bombed in Subic Bay. Aboard were about 1,800 of whom about one-half escaped death, but remained in Japanese hands, many with wounds."

Available records now indicate the largest number of *Hell Ship* voyages, and sinkings, came late in World War II as Allied forces pushed the Japanese off Pacific islands, and back toward Japan. American submarines were sinking large numbers of Japanese merchant ships, and both Army and Navy warplanes were actively attacking Japanese convoys.

It is likely that Richard Kidder and his fellow POWs from Cabanatuan #3 were among the first to suffer a *Hell Ship* trip to Japan, before American submarines began to take a heavy toll on Japanese shipping, and before the Japanese far-east shipping lanes were in range of American bombers.

☆ ☆ ☆

Chapter 9

PRISONER OF WAR – UMEDA BUNSHO

IN JAPAN

The American prisoners, now thrust into the center of a supposedly modern Japanese city, were "shocked" at how backward that nation was. Except for the trains and the city transit system (much more modern and efficient than those they were accustomed to in the United States), the American prisoners considered Osaka to be a very "backward" city. If this were a modern city, they reasoned, what must the rest of the nation be like? The great majority of people they saw in Osaka, or came in contact with each day, were obviously uneducated. They were the "coolies" … the working class. The supervisors, the "honchos", weren't much better.

Japanese were very small people with very black hair. Richard Kidder was one of the smallest of the Americans, but he was almost always taller than his captors. The large Americans, many of them considered a normal size in the United States, appeared to be giants alongside the Japanese, even though the prisoners were mostly skin and bones. But then, the Japanese were not fat, either. They did not have the gaunt appearance of the Americans; their body build was very trim. They were agile, and appeared healthy.

These were a clean people. Their clothing certainly was not stylish, but neither was it ragged. Those who moved heavy goods, like sacks of rice, used a little two-wheeled cart with a tongue, a rig that looked somewhat like a miniature Chinese ricksha. The men, even the older men, had very little, if any, facial hair.

By comparison, the Americans must have appeared to be giant Neanderthals. They were unshaved, and their gaunt appearance, with sunken eyes, gave them a piercing, intense look. Most had on remnants of the uniforms they were wearing when captured. Their body odor was likely unpleasant, for there was no such thing as a full body bath in Japanese POW facilities.

It became apparent very early on that the Japanese civilians were much more fearful of the Japanese military, or anyone in authority for that matter, than were the American prisoners. And their military people often treated their own people with less respect than they treated the Americans. This obvious difference from American expectations could, of course, have been their warrior culture. Or that among the Coolie class anyone with authority liked to display it. Whatever the difference, it was apparent the common man, or especially a woman in Japan, circa 1943, was seriously afraid of Japanese soldiers.

What the American prisoners learned, later on, was that the Japanese Imperial Army "rented" Allied prisoners to Japanese industry to do manual labor. The best of the Japanese work force was in the military, and there was a shortage of labor in the homeland.

When Richard Kidder forced himself to leave the sick bay, he was assigned to a 12-man labor detail that worked for a railroad. Two Japanese coolies, carrying a carved wooden stick that apparently marked them as having authority, and wearing traditional civilian clothing but identified by a black arm band with some Japanese lettering on it, would line their work detail up every morning and count them off. At this point, no American had a name, just an identified work detail and a number. The two guards would walk their detail down the street to public transportation (the subway in Kidder's case), load them aboard and squire them to whatever location the railroad designated. At that point the guards would count them off, and turn them over to a supervisor who worked for the railroad.

The treatment of the American prisoners was totally up to the supervisor. For some prisoner work details from Umeda Bunsho, the supervisor was intentionally cruel, and the work assignment was pure hell. For others the supervisor figured he would get more and better work from his slave POW laborers if he treated them well. It was purely random luck, and in this case Richard Kidder got a break. His railroad supervisor treated his team well ... very well compared to some others.

✻ ✻ ✻

Kidder's work detail loaded and unloaded freight of all kinds, including foodstuffs, and they were able to pilfer small amounts of rice on a regular basis. In raw form the new supply of food was not very advantageous; it needed to be cooked. At this point fortune intervened.

Kidder tells the story this way: "One of our detail (a man named Averill) caught his foot between a boxcar and the loading dock and was slightly injured while working. The Yard Boss didn't want to report it to the Army. So, the railroad people took Averill off the work detail to recuperate in a small wooden shack they had provided to get us out of the cold and rain while we were waiting for the next train to come in. At lunch every day the railroad gave us a small rice ball to supplement the very small ration we got at the barracks."

"Since there was a small pot-bellied stove in the shack, and Averill was already there, we talked them into giving us the raw rice, and letting Averill cook it so we could have a warm lunch. I am sure our two Coolie honchos knew what we were doing, but we were good workers, so they shut their eyes and let us do it."

Other foodstuffs came through, too. Some worked out well, and some did not. Irish potato season came along in 1943, and Kidder's detail loaded and unloaded potatoes constantly. Averill cooked as many as he could every day, but they were always only half done. Says Kidder: "I don't advise anyone to eat their fill of half-baked potatoes and then go out to work shoveling sand. The heartburn is almost unbearable." But the fact is this group of prisoners was now getting enough food to gain strength and improve their health (even though it was still not enough to allow them to gain weight). Staying alive was a major goal for most of the prisoners, for they had seen many of their close friends die, and they were aware not all prisoners were as fortunate as those at Umeda Bunsho.

For some unknown reason, in late Spring, 1943, the Japanese transferred all of the U.S. Army personnel (except the pilot called P-40) out of Umeda Bunsho. The remaining prisoners heard that the soldiers went to Tanagawa to work in the coal mines, a prisoner duty station known to be hazardous, at best, and without any way to get extra food, a starving sentence to a slow death. The U.S. Army prisoners were replaced at Umeda Bunsho with U.S. Navy and Marine personnel. A bit later the Japanese selected the healthiest and strongest from each work group to keep as the work force at Umeda Bunsho. The weaker prisoners were "culled" and sent somewhere else. The Umeda Bunsho contingent never learned where the weaker prisoners were sent, or what happened to them. "Thank goodness," Kidder reminisces, "by then I was considered one of the healthier and stronger POW's."

For the surviving prisoners, the years at Umeda Bunsho were a long, boring blur. Life was an endless repetition of get up early, eat a very small ration of rice, march to the subway, ride to work, WORK, ride and march "home" dog tired, eat another small portion of rice, go to bed. During the first year at Umeda Bunsho the POWs worked six days a week, and had Sunday off. From then on they worked Seven days a week. "It was just as well," Kidder believes. "since if we weren't working, all we could think and talk about was how bad off we were." In many ways it defies logic, but morale was noticeably better without the day off.

There were, however, some memorable moments that broke the monotony. Some would bring laughter; some tears.

One young man lost his mind, a condition most prisoners had only encountered on the *Hell Ship*. The Japanese put him in a bamboo cage in a corner under one of the stairs, where one could hear him jabbering constantly day and night. He didn't say anything intelligible; it was simply gibberish. Then one day when the POWs came back from work, he was no longer there.

One of the highlights most of the POWs remembered was a "visit" from some English prisoners of war. Richard Kidder recalls it this way: "Once the Japanese were transferring a contingent of English prisoners, and they were billeted with us for one night. One young Cockney had been able to hold on to his accordion, and he played for us until we were ordered to go to bed. He played a lot of American songs, many of them our favorites that we would request. When asked why he knew so many American songs, he answered with a very Cockney accent: 'Fats Waller's me favorite, you know.'" This was the second time POW Kidder had been treated to some good music. While a prisoner at Cabanatuan, a man who had been a clarinet player with Artie Shaw's band had managed to hold on to his instrument and played American music, a welcome interlude for the prisoners there.

Then there was the very memorable day that Richard Kidder and his work detail associates got drunk. A boxcar pulled into their railroad station, and Kidder and one other man were told to get inside the car and hand out the boxes to be stacked on the dock. They had no idea what was in the boxes, but after a few were handed down the handlers heard glass rattle inside a box, and noticed (and smelled) liquid that was staining the outside of that particular box. It was obviously beer. After that, they would set a box aside; open the top of the box, uncap a beer and drink it; break the beer bottle and place the broken glass back in its slot inside the box; and hand it out to be stacked. And as one said, they found a way to "share the wealth". For one day, at least, there was one more happy, and drunk, prisoner of war work detail. In retrospect, the surprising thing was that the Japanese guards did not understand what was happening. Or maybe they did, and chose to do nothing about it.

And don't forget the garlic episode. The American prisoners were having constant problems with beri-beri, a disease caused by lack of Vitamin B1, characterized by nerve disorders. One of the American prisoners insisted if they could get, and eat, garlic it would cure beri-beri. Then came a day when Kidder's work detail was unloading a railroad car, and a few bags of garlic appeared. The Americans managed to hide a whole bag at the railroad warehouse. Every day for several weeks, they would pop a small garlic bud in their mouth, chew it up, and swallow it. The garlic "treatment" did not help the beri-beri, but it did help in another way. When the two Coolies who guarded the 12-man work detail took them from Umeda Bunsho to their work place, they would simply shove them in the door of a subway car and crowd the Japanese passengers together tightly enough to make room. The American prisoners were in very close proximity to the Japanese civilians, but the prisoners began to realize they had more room than usual. Then one day a petite and sophisticated Japanese lady held her nose and grimaced when the Americans started to board, and said something that sounded like Kuk-sui and most of the other Japanese passengers laughed. The POW's were told later that translated to "you stink." They realized if their usual body odor was not enough, now the garlic. The prisoners laughed for days about that one, fully convinced the word was spreading around Osaka that Americans not only stunk from body odor, but they also had very bad breath. It was a welcome interlude, for these prisoners had very little to laugh about.

World War II was an era in which nicknames were in vogue among Americans, and the POWs joined right in to the fad. Flyboys named their airplanes, and were allowed to paint those very un-military names on military planes. Generals were fondly referred to as "Skinny" or "Old Blood and Guts." The commander-in-chief was neither referred to by name nor as the president – he was FDR. Nicknames were part of the culture of the times. That was true of the POWs, too, but with a different twist.

Richard Kidder knew two Japanese by their real names. The two guards assigned to his work detail were Yamoto and Mitah. After two years together that was what the American prisoners called them, and by comparison with other guards they were decent people worthy of some extra respect.

But everybody else had a nickname, and when it was mentioned all the POWs knew who it belonged to. Richard Kidder especially remembers "Bruno the Dog" and "Pluto." Dr. Bumgarner remembered "Dopey", "Groucho", and "Stumpy" who had lost part of one arm. The commander of Cabanatuan #3 when Richard Kidder was there, Lt. Col. Masao Mori, was referred to as "Bamboo Mori", and the officer under him who was most disliked was "Slime." Col. Irvin Alexander, who wrote *Surviving Bataan and Beyond*, remembers "Hammer Head", "Fish Eyes", "Web Foot", and "Hog Jaw." And then there were "Laughing Boy", "Donald Duck" and "Air Raid." Many at Cabanatuan remembered "Speedo." Every time he walked near a work detail, he would admonish them to work harder with the command "speedo." As one POW is quoted as saying, "When you live with them all the time, you've got to call them something."

☆ ☆ ☆

Most American prisoners had a vivid memory of some personal incident that stood out in their minds, but not necessarily in everyone's. For many the incident was dramatic. The death of a friend, or the transfer of a friend for an unknown reason, or a friend never heard from again. Or seeing big city streets with no automobiles in sight. Or the truck with a steam engine, and a coolie building a fire under it to get the steam started. Unusual things left strong memories.

For Richard Kidder this one stands out still; "One night during evening roll call, a fellow opposite from where I was standing began pantomiming. It was so funny I couldn't help but laugh. As could be expected, the Japanese guard taking roll call came into our room at that moment. He chewed me out (even though I did not know what he said; it was obvious what he meant). But it didn't end there. After muster he called me over to the guard shack. He stood me at attention and began slapping me, first with one hand and then the other. I was not aware that a small man, no bigger than me, could slap so hard. My face was swollen, and I was in pain for a number of days." Years later Richard Kidder remembered this incident and said: "I used to say I would love to be in a room with this man for a few minutes to get in some licks of my own, but now I can't even remember his name." Time heals a lot of things, but it doesn't always wipe out painful memories.

☆ ☆ ☆

It was May 6, 1944, and Richard Kidder had been a prisoner of the Japanese for two full years. Two days before, on May 4, he had a totally uneventful birthday. In some ways it was better than two years previously, when he spent his birthday in a foxhole on Corregidor wondering if the next artillery shell had his name on it. On this birthday, he was still a slave in Japan, working on the railroad, but somewhat safe. The haunting question remained: for how long?

One of the great challenges for these prisoners of war was maintaining their morale and their hope. For the first few weeks of their captivity this had not been an issue. But as their imprisonment extended past year one, and then year two; and now with the third year beginning, maintaining hope, and thus morale, became a personal challenge.

Adding to the mental anguish was the fact these prisoners had no clue about what was happening in the war itself. The last news they had heard was just before their capture, and at that time the Japanese were chalking up an unbroken string of stunning victories. This enemy was almost to Australia when Corregidor fell, and Kidder and his fellow POWs were captured.

Since they were still prisoners, they instinctively knew the war was still going on. They had absolute faith that America would never abandon them … would never surrender. Each person in Kidder's POW contingent developed his own way of coping with his situation, and almost all adopted the belief that "Hope Has No Limit." For some their personal goal was to hold out for six more months, and then it would be over. When it failed to happen, they simply extended it another six months. Kidder worked on a one-year timetable. "Hang in there another year, and we'll be going home." One of the members of his group was more creative, and had the goal of "Golden Gate in' 48". Even in their darkest days, they never lost a firm belief that America would prevail in this war, and that they would go home as victors. They were Americans, and for Americans "hope had no limit."

✴ ✴ ✴

If these prisoners of the Japanese had been privy to the same newsreels the Americans were seeing in their theaters back home, they would have been pleased ... even excited ... with the direction World War II was taking, both in Europe and in the Pacific in the Spring of 1944.

They would have been thrilled to know that the die-hard defense of Bataan, and especially the extra 27 days it took the Japanese to dislodge these prisoners from Corregidor, had slowed the Japanese Imperial Army down and seriously thrown them off of their invasion timetable.

More important, the extra days had given the U.S. Navy time to get its carrier task forces in place. On 7–8 May, 1942, while these POWs were still being moved to Cabanatuan #3 in the Philippines, the Japanese had moved a massive invasion force, protected by a carrier force, toward Port Moresby in southern New Guinea. The Japanese fleet was intercepted by an American naval force built around the aircraft carriers USS Lexington and USS Yorktown, and the Battle of the Coral Sea was underway, starting a new era in naval warfare. It was a major battle dominated by aircraft, a battle in which the two fleets fought an entire engagement without surface ships exchanging a single shot. The U.S. Navy sank a Japanese light cruiser and the aircraft carrier Shoho. At the same time, the U.S. lost a destroyer, an oiler, and the aircraft carrier USS Lexington. The Japanese commanders turned back, fearing the disaster possible if American airplanes began sinking the Japanese ships filled with soldiers. The exciting result of this battle was that the entire Japanese juggernaut moving toward Australia was stopped cold.

A month later an American aircraft carrier task force which included the USS Yorktown, USS Enterprise and USS Hornet squared off in the Battle of Midway against a Japanese carrier fleet led by Admiral Isoroku Yamamota, the architect of the Pearl Harbor attack, and soundly defeated them. The American navy sank three main-line Japanese carriers the first day: the Soru, Kaga and Akagi. And the next day a submarine finished off a wounded carrier, the Hiryu. The U.S. Navy lost the USS Yorktown. Many historians consider the Battle of Midway to be the turning point in the war in the Pacific.

Had they known about it, these American prisoners would have been especially thrilled about General Doolittle's air raid on Tokyo. They likely would have been astounded at the number of American troops pushing the Japanese off of Pacific islands, back toward Japan itself. And with the airlift flying the hump from India, allowing Chinese and American forces to keep the Japanese tied up in China. They would have been awe-struck at the number of new ships and airplanes sent to the Pacific by the American industrial machine.

But, Richard Kidder and his fellow American POWs, now slaves in the Japanese homeland, had no word about the progress of the war, either in Europe or the Pacific. One of the strategies used by the Japanese was to keep all prisoners of war totally in the dark so far as news was concerned. So far they had been very successful. This was about to change.

✽ ✽ ✽

Chapter 10

GOOD NEWS FILTERS IN

Time goes oh-so-slowly when one is a prisoner of war, doing the same dreary tasks day-after-day with no inkling of what is going on in the outside world. But as 1944 began, with Richard Kidder and his fellow POWs still prisoners of war at Umeda Bunsho, in Osaka, on the mainland of Japan, the American prisoners began to get clues that American forces were moving up the islands toward Japan, and winning big sea battles to boot.

At first it was little things that various POWs picked up while out among the local Japanese citizens on their work details. But there was always a question about these reports: is this a fact, or is it rumor? It sounded like the United States was winning some battles on islands in the Pacific, but the names of the islands were unfamiliar. What about islands these prisoners knew about? What about the Philippines? What about Formosa? China?

Something was happening on some islands named Mariana and Saipan, for the POWs heard them mentioned. These were unfamiliar names to Kidder and his POW friends. But had they just known, they would have been joyous. On June 15, 1944, (just as Eisenhower was consolidating his Normandy beachhead in Europe) Admiral Nimitz' forces hit Saipan in the Mariana Islands with a force that comprised 535 ships and 127,000 men – two-thirds of them marines. The landings triggered the most intensive aircraft carrier battle of the war, and it became known in America as the "Great Marianas Turkey Shoot." The United States lost 130 airplanes in that action, but the Japanese lost more than 500 airplanes and three of their mainline aircraft carriers. The importance of Saipan Island, in the Marianas, was obvious to both American and Japanese leaders; it was in bombing range of Japan for the new B-29 bombers now being turned out in volume by the American industrial complex.

Living in the midst of an enemy city, and coming in daily contact with the Japanese people, was a bit weird. Even the difference in languages could not totally conceal the concern of the Japanese civilians. At first one of the POWs would hear something he could translate, and then another would hear something else, but they all added to the hope that the Americans were winning the war in the Pacific.

For instance, there was the young American POW who started a conversation, in English, with an attractive young Japanese girl and talked with her regularly while on the subway. She almost always took the same subway as this POW group. She was taking English in school, she said, and wanted to practice the language. They had a number of conversations, and even seemed to enjoy each other's lively, even flirtatious, comments in English. English that was good enough for the other POWs to understand. Then one day that American prisoner was transferred out of Umeda Bunsho, and that work detail never again saw the young lady. She did not divulge anything specifically, but had indicated the war was not going well with the Japanese.

Then in the fall of 1944 the big American bombers, the B-29s, began to fire bomb Japanese cities, an action the rulers of Japan could not hide. Although the Umeda area of Osaka was not severely damaged, much of the rest of the city was. Going to work one day, Kidder's work detail saw a new kind of damaged equipment being displayed in a small shopping area, and they were proudly told it was from a big U.S. B-29 bomber that had been shot down. The American POWs were not familiar with B-29s. The planes flew so high all they could see were the vapor trails – the contrails – but it was confirmation that the Americans were, indeed, bombing Japan. The Americans had to be getting closer. And another day Richard Kidder saw a Japanese Zero fighter climb almost straight up until it went out of sight approaching visible contrails. Something was going on, that much was certain.

One of the Umeda Bunsho POWs worked in a group with a Korean man, and the American began to trade his rice to the Korean for copies of an English-language newspaper published in Tokyo. The newspaper itself was a great curiosity to the POWs; why an English language newspaper in Japan? The POWs had been told Imperial Japan had tight control of its press, and thus any newspaper in Japan would print only what the leaders wanted to print. But in time, it became clear that the news in this paper was reasonably accurate in its coverage of the war. The prisoners enjoyed the fact that every time a Japanese-held island was lost to the Americans it was called a "strategic withdrawal." The POWs were careful never to openly bring the newspaper back to the prison, believing if the Japanese discovered it, the incident could lead to trouble ... even possibly executions. It was from this newspaper that the Americans first learned of D-Day in Europe ... a bit of news that raised their hopes ... maybe too high, for nothing changed immediately.

But their best source of outside information, and a source that served them well until they were liberated, was one of their own Marines, a Cajun from South Louisiana. He had been raised speaking both English and French, but also was one of those people who simply had a knack for learning languages. He had been in China, and had learned Chinese by talking to the natives. Now that he had been in Japanese prison camps for two-plus years, he had become proficient in speaking the Japanese language. Even the Japanese guards used him at times as their interpreter. His translations were usually better than those of their own interpreter. Very often the Japanese guards had a radio in their guard shack, or nearby, so they could hear the daily news, and this Marine found ways to get close enough to hear the news reports. In due time he began to get a good picture of the war in the Pacific, and of the fact the Americans were steadily pushing ever closer to Japan, while the Japanese were making "strategic withdrawals" back toward their homeland.

As Richard Kidder approached the end of his third year of captivity, the POWs in his contingent were beginning to stay abreast of the news about the war in the Pacific, and in their eyes that news was generally good.

It is easier to hang on, they agreed, when you think you can see light at the end of the tunnel.

✼ ✼ ✼

Chapter 11

THE VISE TIGHTENS ON MAINLAND JAPAN

It was June 15, 1944, that forty-seven of the big, new B-29 bombers of the United States Army Air Force revved up their engines on an airport in mainland China, and took off to bomb the Imperial Iron and Steel Works at Yawata on the Japanese mainland. It was the first bombing raid on Japan itself since Doolittle's daring flight early in 1942, and it marked the beginning of the battle for Japan itself. Machinists, like Richard Kidder, who had worked in the shop of a submarine tender, fully understood the symbolism: a vise WAS tightening on Japan, from China on one side and from the islands of the Pacific on the other.

Yawata was due west of Richard Kidder's POW camp in Osaka, and was located on the western side of Japan, facing the Korea Straight that joins the Yellow Sea to the Sea of Japan. Near a coal mining section, Yawata was a major steel producer in an industrial region that included Hiroshima and Nagasaki, two cities practically unheard of outside Japan at that time.

Then in July 1944, American forces secured Saipan and its airfield in the Marianna Islands, placing Japan in range for

B-29s from that direction. To deny the Japanese an airfield from which their Zero fighters could intercept the B-29s en route to Japan, and to provide an emergency airfield for B-29s that had been damaged, the U.S. needed to take little Iwo Jima island, located about half way between Saipan and Tokyo. The Marine landings promptly began, starting one of the bloodiest and costliest battles of the entire war. Supplying Saipan with bombs, fuel and supplies from the United States was much easier, and much more efficient, than supplying bases in China.

Things were happening very rapidly in late 1944 and early 1945, mostly good for the United States so far as the progress of the war was concerned, yet disturbing in the cost of American lives. But America was committed. It planned to win this war unconditionally.

The big news back home in this era was that MacArthur had returned to the Philippines. It was an important victory, both from a battlefield standpoint and to boost morale throughout the Allied world. But in the Pacific Theater of War the closer the Allied forces came to Japan, the more ferocious the Japanese defenders fought. The Americans opened their campaign to retake the Philippines with a landing on Leyte island. Japanese defenders there sacrificed virtually all of their garrison of 50,000 troops trying to stop the invasion. One eye-witness of this battle said: "It appeared the Japanese were fighting to die; and the Americans were fighting to live." American casualties totaled 3,504, and the Americans won the battle.

Japan also introduced the Kamikaze bombers, flown by suicide pilots who flew their bomb-laden planes all the way to their target. They were especially effective against America's big ships. The Americans had a hard time understanding a culture in which people would intentionally, and proudly, kill themselves in order to damage an enemy target.

The United States was just as determined to win, although it seems fair to say this country sacrificed technology and industry-produced war goods rather than human lives ... even though the cost in lives was high.

POW Richard Kidder and his fellow shipmates from the USS Canopus no doubt sensed that the United States was winning one battle that was hardly mentioned in the American press, and not at all in Japan – the American submarine blockade of Japan. During 1943 alone, the "silent service", operating in Japanese waters, sunk 22 enemy warships and 296 merchant ships. The island homeland of Japan was almost totally dependent on shipments for many of its critical supplies, among them oil and food. That was the reason Japan had started this war in the first place. By the summer of 1945, the shipping lifeline serving Japan was virtually shut down.

✵ ✵ ✵

Many of the events that made top headlines in America went unknown at the time among the American prisoners of war in Japan. But one thing known by the POWs, and everybody else in the Japanese homeland, was the new incendiary bombs, the fire bombs, being delivered by the American B-29 bombers.

One military history chronicled it this way, "Starting in February 1945, employing a new bomb containing magnesium and jellied gasoline, (B-29) bombers burned out factories, docks, urban areas, and Tokyo itself. ... On the night of March 9–10 (1945), just after midnight, the pounding of Tokyo started amid a high wind. Within half an hour, the resulting fires had flamed wholly out of control." The Tokyo fire department later estimated that single air raid killed 97,000 people, injured 125,000 and left 1,200,000 homeless. The targets were Japan's largest cities: Tokyo, Nagoya, Kobe and Osaka. There was hope in some Allied quarters that the fire bombings would bring Japan to its knees; would cause it to surrender. But it soon became evident that the Japanese planned to fight to the death, no mater what the cost. America was planning its invasion of mainland Japan for late fall or early winter, 1945. Troops were already being transferred from Europe to the Pacific.

Although Osaka was one of the main targets of the fire bombing, the Umeda section, for the most part, was spared. Kidder saw little fire-bomb damage in his daily travel to the railroad station, but he and his fellow POWs were very perceptive about the reason they were suddenly transferred out of Osaka, and moved across the Japanese island of Honshu to a small seaport town named Tsuraga. The POWs reasoned the American bombing was having at least one desired affect in that "…their rail traffic was greatly hampered," and "… there was less work for us (in Osaka), or they needed us more someplace else where the bombing was not as intense." Whatever the reason, the entire POW contingent was put on a train and shipped to Tsuraga where they would load and unload ships.

✯ ✯ ✯

It had been three full years since Richard Kidder and his fellow U.S. troops had been surrendered on Corregidor, in the Philippines, and as springtime began to blossom in Japan, things were looking up for these POWs. Their new barracks was a large building just across from the dock and warehouse, so they didn't have the every day march to and from their work station. It was not as comfortable as barracks they would have had in America, of course, but excellent by Japanese standards. The POW group became stevedores, unloading bags of soybeans from ships, and stacking them in the warehouse. Then a train would pull in, and the bags of soybeans were transferred from the warehouse to boxcars. The POWs' meager rice ration was now mixed with pilfered soybeans, and the cooked mixture gave these POWs the best diet they had received in more than three years. Yes, cooked. It's amazing what the American POWs had learned to accomplish in three years of captivity.

Although most conditions in Tsuraga were improvements over their other prisons, there was one major difference: the guards were much tougher. The guards at Umeda had been Reservists ... men too old or too infirmed for front-line duty. Some had fought in the war with China, but whatever their background, they had been reasonably lenient in their treatment of prisoners. The guards in Tsuraga were regular Army. Some had fought the Americans in the islands of the South Pacific, and were back in Japan because the Americans had won the battle and pushed them off of that island. They were very rigid, very military and very unforgiving. Even so, these POWs later learned that "... the guards we had (at Tsuraga) were not nearly as cruel as in some other prison camps."

Instinctively, these Americans knew the battle for Japan was underway, in the air at least. Vapor trails would often fill the morning sky, and the POWs Cajun interpreter was reporting that the B-29s were methodically fire-bombing cities, including

Tokyo. He was able to regularly get in range of a Japanese radio, and became a "newscaster" for the entire unit.

The POWs had enjoyed their new barracks for several weeks, but then the seaport town of Tsuraga became a designated target for the B-29s and their fire-bombs. The bombs effectively hit the town, but missed the warehouse, hit the barracks, and burned it flat to the ground. Only one American was injured; he had a finger burned off.

The prisoners were moved into the warehouse itself, sleeping on the dirt floor and living at the end opposite where the soybeans were usually stacked. It wasn't a bad arrangement. These prisoners had seen worse, and as the weeks went by it appeared this was to be their permanent residence.

It was while they were living in the warehouse that a flight of U.S. Navy fighter-bombers came through at treetop level, strafing the dock, the warehouse and everything around it. The second the POWs realized what was happening, they raced to an adjacent field and dived behind a stone fence. Bullets were flying everywhere. Kidder remembers it this way: "We were all excited, but we had all been under this kind of fire before, and we knew American bullets could kill you just as quickly as Japanese. Along with the other POWs I dived behind that wall. But would you believe that one of our POWs stood on top of that wall during the entire strafing, waving his hat and cheering the fighters on. Happy or not, my Mama didn't raise any crazy chillun." Luckily, no Americans were hurt.

This was a major morale-booster for the prisoners. No longer was the war on Japan just being carried out by long-range bombers; these planes meant there was an American aircraft carrier somewhere nearby. The POWs knew something good was happening, and they showed it, sort of like a pro football player showboating in the end zone after making a touchdown.

The Japanese guards were not pleased with the strafing event to begin with, but the POWs enthusiasm obviously made them mad. They moved the entire contingent out of the warehouse, and about five miles out in the country, to live in an abandoned brick kiln. It was a ramshackle structure with a dirt floor, few remaining walls, and a leaky roof.

After that, the POWs had to get up very early in the morning; walk the five miles to the warehouse; work all day; and at dark start their walk back to their "quarters." This dull day-in day-out routine continued for the rest of the summer.

"Then one day our Cajun interpreter told us a Coolie was talking about this huge bomb the Americans had dropped. He did not call it an atomic bomb, and he did not say where it had been dropped," Kidder remembers. "The version we got was that the U.S. had dropped a bomb that wiped out an entire city, tearing down or burning all the buildings, and killing all the inhabitants. We didn't believe it. We thought panic had set in among the homeland Japanese. We had lived through intense bombings on Bataan and Corregidor, and knew from personal experience that if you were lying in a small ditch you could be very close to where a bomb hit, and not be hurt, except for the ringing in your ears. If you were running or standing, that was a different story."

Kidder continues: "We did not hear about the second bomb, but not too long after (the news of the first bomb), we were called in from work and marched back to the brick kiln. We knew something was radically wrong (for the Japanese). In three-years-and-four-months (of captivity), we had never knocked off from work in the middle of the day."

That evening, the POWs trusty Creole interpreter heard the news on the guard house radio: JAPAN WAS SURRENDERING! It certainly sounded like the war was over, but the POWs took caution not to start celebrating yet. Who knew what the Japanese had in store. In all of these Americans' experience during the war, no Japanese soldier had hesitated to kill an American if given the chance. Also, many American prisoners had heard a rumor that the Japanese Army had a standing order to kill all American prisoners of war the moment the first boot from an American invasion force stepped on the soil of mainland Japan. It may have been one of those whispered rumors that runs the rounds, or maybe speculation. But to American POWs that sounded much more like a thing the Japanese would do than to simply give up. (A concern that the Japanese might execute all POWs was not only found among the prisoners; it went all the way to the high command in Washington.)

"We spent the night with a sense of dread," Kidder recalls. But nothing happened.

The next morning the guards packed their things, and walked off. "They just left us sitting there, all alone," Kidder says. There was great hope, and muted excitement. Was the war really over? It looked that way. But there was great anxiety, too. Here was a small contingent of American troops, unarmed and vulnerable, isolated deep within a country known for harsh treatment of its enemies. One could not help but think of the irony of surviving a brutal war, and three years as a slave laborer for the enemy, and then on the day of victory to lose it all.

The word went out to all POW groups in Japan: stay where you are. We will come to you. There is debate about how they got that word. Some say they heard it on Japanese radio. Others say leaflets were dropped. Most believe both things happened. But they do know that somehow they were told to place white POW markers on top of the buildings in which they were located, and to sit tight till someone came to get them.

For a day or so nothing appeared to change, and then things began to happen in a somewhat orderly way. The POWs left the brick kiln, returned to Tsuraga and moved into a large, roomy building (where they stayed until repatriated). Somehow, the message was confirmed to sit tight until their return could be arranged. There was still concern that die-hard Japanese might take advantage of this small, unarmed contingent of Americans and kill them.

It took a while to sink in, but now these prisoners ... some of the first American prisoners of World War II ... knew the war was finally over, and that America and its allies had won. They were ready to go home, but they would spend four weeks ... closer to five weeks, really ...in Tsuraga before good things began to happen. The Japanese had Prisoner-of-War forced labor groups scattered all over the mainland. Rounding them up had a very high priority for the Americans, but it was not an easy job in a bomb-ravaged country.

Japan surrendered on August 14, 1945. The unconditional surrender was made official September 2, 1945, when documents were signed on the deck of the battleship Missouri, anchored in Tokyo Bay.

✳ ✳ ✳

Chapter 12

WANT TO GO HOME, SAILOR?

It was a huge airplane, certainly the largest these Americans had ever seen, flying low and surprisingly slow as it approached Tsuraga from over the inland mountains. The POWs figured it was one of the new B-29s. It just had to be. They had heard about the big bombers, of course, but the only evidence of the big plane they had seen before were the vapor trails. This new addition to the American arsenal was always too high to identify the airplane causing the white trails in the sky.

Suddenly the big plane started dropping things. The tumbling items falling from the sky didn't look like bombs, and sure enough they weren't. They were fifty-five gallon drums filled with food and goodies, and these packages were scattered across an open space near the building on which the prisoners had spelled out a white POW. It was like Christmas in Tsuraga. It wasn't just the food, although that was welcome. This was "friendly fire", and it eased their concerns about being a "lost tribe" of Americans in an unfriendly land.

"At least somebody knew we existed," Kidder said, "and they knew where we were." These POWs now had reasonably comfortable living conditions and food. The orders were still to sit tight; someone would come get them.

A week went by. Then another. And another. After the war it was learned the occupying forces first sought out the larger prison camps, and those closest to the large port cities on the east coast of Japan. Obviously, they were easier to get to. Kidder's group of American POWs was relatively small, out of the way, and located on the west coast of Japan.

Kidder recalls: "We walked around town at will, but it was weird. I didn't see a Japanese civilian all during the time we were there. I think they were afraid of us. A good bit of damage had been done by fire bombs. We were impatient, ready to get going, but still believed the best thing to do was to stay put … to wait for help to come to us."

One small group, however, decided to strike out on its own. They went to the railroad station and told the people there General MacArthur had sent for them, and got on a train, probably headed for Tokyo. "I heard later," Kidder laughed, "that they didn't go all the way. They got off the train at some beautiful resort town high in the mountains, commandeered a resort hotel (again in the name of MacArthur) and stayed there until retrieved by American troops." What a way to end the war.

At the end of the fourth week, probably closer to the fifth, a Canadian Major and a Sergeant drove into town in a jeep and found the POWs. He checked to be sure all were okay, then took the traditional name/rank/and serial number. He said he would arrange transportation for them to Yokohama, and be back ASAP (as soon as possible). Eventually the Canadian major returned, and had the POWs loaded on a train. The group traveled all night, and arrived in Yokohama the next morning.

Yokohama was a bee hive of activity. Americans were all over the place, but they were well organized and efficient. Kidder and his fellow POWs were checked in at a very large, metal building ... apparently a newly-erected Quonset hut. They took a shower, got new Navy clothing, and took a "bunch" of shots. This was Kidder's first experience seeing enlisted females in service, except for nurses. "It was disconcerting," he said, "to be told by them: 'drop your pants and bend over, sailor'. And if that wasn't degrading enough, a shot in the buttocks soon followed."

Several medical people told Kidder and his group they were "among the cleanest and healthiest looking prisoners" they had encountered. It was the first time Kidder realized how fortunate they had been to draw assignments that allowed them to pilfer extra food, and how much the extra nourishment from the soybeans had meant to them the past few months.

After a rather thorough interrogation, Kidder was placed aboard a boat and taken out to a battleship. Battleships needed deep water in which to anchor, and Kidder remembers the shuttle went by a number of smaller ships and took a good while to reach its destination. It was the first time he had been on a ship since the devastating experience when he was stuffed in the hold of a hot freighter, and as a prisoner taken from the Philippines to Yokohama, the port he was now in. He came aboard in time to get his fill of "good old American chow."

At that moment Kidder was not impressed that the battleship he had been taken to was the USS Missouri, for he did not know where the Japanese surrender ceremony that officially ended World War II had been held. But in later years it was pleasing to know he had stood on the deck, even the spot, where that significant ceremony had been held.

That evening, before dark, he went topside to look around, and saw the most amazing sight any sailor could imagine. "As far as I could see, probably 15 miles out to sea, we were surrounded by warships: battleships, carriers, cruisers, destroyers, and other vessels that I couldn't identify. The entire American and British Asiatic fleets were there. I am sure this was the largest armada of seagoing vessels ever assembled. There may have been more ships at D-Day. Some insist that is so. But many of those were landing craft, not intended for long trips in the open ocean. These were not landing craft; these were warships."

Kidder was assigned a bunk in the enlisted quarters, and for the first time since the Canopus was scuttled more than three years prior, he climbed into a "real bunk." He was asleep almost immediately.

It was in the middle of the night, probably about 3 a.m., that this friendly U.S. sailor gently shook Richard Kidder awake, and said softly: "Want to go home, sailor? Would you like to go home?"

✲ ✲ ✲

Kidder was delivered to the airport, and placed on a twin engine transport plane, probably a Navy version of the DC-3. They flew through the outer edge of a typhoon where everybody was bounced around till they got air sick, until finally the pilot decided it was too rough and landed at Iwo Jima for the night.

The next day the plane flew on to Guam. Kidder spent about 10 days on Guam "...until the doctors were pretty sure we didn't have any communicable disease. We also continued taking shots. I'm still not sure what all of those shots were about," Kidder comments.

The only highlight of the long trip going home across the Pacific was when he got to attend a real, live Bob Hope Show on Guam.

In due time he was put on a plane to San Francisco where he was checked in at the San Francisco Naval Hospital. Although he was in better physical condition than many of the other prisoners of the Japanese, he still showed the symptoms of his ordeal. He weighed about 90 pounds. But he was tough ... that he did not have to prove.

The Red Cross furnished Kidder with a free phone call home. They helped him find his mother's phone number in Los Angeles, and placed the call. Kidder remembers it this way: "My sister answered the phone and I recognized her voice so I said 'hello, sis'. Her reply was 'who is this sissing me?' When I told her, she let out a scream and called the family to the phone. The entire family was there including two I didn't know and had never met, my sister's husband and my older brother's wife. I told them where I was, and my mother kept repeating: 'you stay right there; we are on our way. You stay right there; we are on our way.'" The whole family drove immediately to San Francisco. Kidder had liberty so the newly reunited family got a couple of motel rooms "and talked the night away."

The next morning Kidder was given orders to the Long Beach Naval Hospital, so he rode there with the family caravan. "When I reported in to the hospital, the first thing I was told was to buy a new uniform; that I was now a Chief Petty Officer, not a first class." Becoming a Chief started a long string of backdated promotions that would have happened in a timely manner had he not been a prisoner of war. He had been a first class petty officer while on the Canopus, and had been recommended for Warrant Carpenter, but had become a prisoner before that promotion came through. On March 28, 1946, his recommendation for Warrant officer caught up with him. He never actually served as a Warrant Carpenter, but his date of rank was established as June 1, 1942. He was commissioned an Ensign on July 16, 1942, to rank from October 1, 1943. Then he was appointed a Lieutenant (junior grade) on September 26, 1946, to rank from January 1, 1945. Not only did the promotions catch up with him, but he also got back pay according to date of rank.

It was late fall 1945. The United States of America and her Allies had just won the largest, costliest war in the history of man. And now Richard Kidder, and millions of other GIs who were "every day Americans", who had paid the price to maintain freedom and survived, were home. As the year 2000 rolled around, they would be called "The Greatest Generation", not only for the price they paid during World War II, but also for what they accomplished afterward.

Chapter 13

A COMMON AMERICAN

OF UNCOMMON VALOR

Richard Kidder spent the next three months escorting his mother across America to visit relatives – San Antonio, Nashville, Little Rock. While in Arkansas, he visited Winchester to look up a high school girl friend. She was married, it turned out, but while there he met her older sister, Edith Smith. He took her and her two cousins to Pine Bluff for dinner and dancing. A courtship ensued.

Edith Smith and Ensign Richard Kidder were married in October, 1946, while he was assigned to the Naval Repair Base in New Orleans. He served short tours of duty in Norfolk, Virginia, where their first daughter was born; in Argentia, Newfoundland, and Key West, Florida, where their second daughter was born. During the Korean War he was sent back to the Pacific, and for a while was stationed in Manila Bay. Eventually he returned to San Diego. He was promoted to Lieutenant and then to Lt. Commander, and received one of the Navy's most respected assignments, especially for an officer who has specialized, when he was made the commanding officer of an ARD, a seagoing floating drydock. On May 31, 1959, he retired.

The Kidders stayed in San Diego and these years marked a happy time. The new civilian life style was very rewarding, especially for Richard Kidder. He did something he had always longed to do. He went to San Diego State University, getting first a Bachelors degree in mathematics education, and then a Masters degree. He had always liked to read, always respected education, and when he got a job teaching high school math he found it to be a particularly pleasing vocation. He and Edith acquired a home, and enjoyed raising their two daughters. Richard attended three Philippine Prisoner of War conventions, and a reunion of the Canopus, where he learned the man he took to the hospital on that fateful day on Corregidor had survived. Richard Kidder and his family were living the American Dream.

Then in August, 1966, his world fell apart. The Kidder family had decided to go on vacation to Yosemite National Park. The older daughter, Stephanie, had a job as an organist in a local church, so the family packed early and left as soon as services were over. Stephanie was driving. Barbara, the younger daughter, was in the front seat with her. Richard and Edith were in the back seat. The wreck totally mangled the car. Kidder's wife and both daughters were killed. Stephanie was almost 19. Babs, as she was called, was almost 16. It took Richard more than a year to gain a reasonable physical recovery from his injuries.

Richard Kidder, understandably, was devastated. It took him more than five years to get his life going again, but eventually he did, and began a new career, teaching mathematics at the college level. An opening was advertised at the University of

Tennessee in Chattanooga. Feeling he would do well to make a change, and go back east, he applied for, and received, the job. While in Chattanooga he decided to study for his doctorate. He applied for a graduate fellowship, was accepted, and went to the University of Georgia, in Athens.

There he met Betty Brewer, who was working in the finance department at the University. "I did not believe I could fall in love again," Richard said, "but I did." They were married in 1972. After receiving his doctorate in mathematics education, Richard then joined the faculty at Longwood College in Farmville, Virginia, where he and Betty spent 14 happy years, Richard teaching and Betty working as a stockbroker. At age 68 Richard retired, and the couple moved back to North Georgia. They located in Jefferson, Georgia, located between Athens and Gainesville. There they made friends, and life was good again.

Then, Betty's health failed her, first because of breast cancer and then with Parkinson's disease. The couple moved to Lanier Village Estates, a continuing care retirement resort located on the shores of Lake Lanier, near Gainesville, Georgia. Betty died December 29, 2004.

That is where, at this writing in 2007, Richard Kidder insists he is not a hero, but just an everyday, common American who is a survivor … and where his neighbors will remind you that America is kept free by men like Richard Kidder, by Common Americans of Uncommon Valor.

ENDNOTES

Research for this work began with Richard Kidder, and notes he had made for a presentation to a granddaughter's class at her school. This was followed with a series of interviews by the author over several months in 2006–07. While Richard Kidder is the heart of the story, it was felt the biography would be more meaningful if it were presented in context with the great events of World War II in the Pacific.

National Geographic. Map supplement. Dec. 1991, page 50A. Vol 180 No. 6 – World War II. A timeline was established using the National Geographic map "World War II Asia and the Pacific" which shows dates when territory was taken by the Japanese and dates taken back by the Allies. This map also shows dates and locations of major naval battles and major ships lost by both Japan and the U.S. This was supplemented with a detailed timeline on Wikipedia — Pacific War.

Bailey, Jennifer L.U.S. Army Center of Military History. CMH Pub 72–3. On the 50th anniversary of Victory in World War II, the Department of Defense published a series of booklets about the major battles of that war. The Booklet on the battle for the Philippines 1941–42 gives an excellent summary of the period in which Richard Kidder served there.

Wikipedia (the free internet encyclopedia) was used extensively for general information. However, when such information was used, this author attempted to verify from another source. (NOTE: the Wikipedia information proved to be very accurate).

The U. S Military Academy at West Point. Department of History. General information about World War II in the Pacific.

West Point Atlas with 50 WW II maps, including the map showing the Japanese Centrifugal strategy. <www.dean.usma.edu/HISTORY/web03/atlasses/ww2>

West Point. Register of Graduates of the U.S. Military Academy, 2000 edition.

United States Naval Institute, Annapolis, MD. The photograph of the U.S.S. Canopus, and the rights to use it in this work, was purchased from this non-government organization.

Roscoe, Theodore. United States SUBMARINE OPERATIONS in World War II, Naval Institute Press, Annapolis, MD. (Ninth printing, 1972). Much of the information about submarine operations in the Pacific was either gathered or verified from this 577 page book loaned to this author by Victor L. Lee, who served on submarines in the far east in World War II. This was the first book in the U.S. Naval Institutes' World War II history series.

Parkinson, James W. and Benson, Lee. *Soldier Slaves*. Naval Institute Press. 2006.

Michno, Gregory F., *Death on the Hellships*. Naval Institute Press: Annapolis, MD, 2001.

Boyle, David. *World War II: A Photographic History*. Metro Books, 2001. Especially the chapter "Japanese Atrocities: The Crimes of the Empire of the Sun."

Boyle David. *Britain at War*. Information on Hell Ships. <http://www.britain-at-war.org.uk/Hell_ships/index.htm>

Sulzberger, C. L. *The American Heritage Picture History of World War II*. American Heritage Publishing Co. Distributed by Simon and Schuster, Inc. 1966. p 161–63, p 173, p 149.

Gladwin, Lee A. *Prologue Magazine.* Winter 2003. Vol. 35 No. 4. Archival Services Branch, Center for electronics records. National Archives and Records Administration.

Bumgarner, John R. *Parade of the Dead – A. U.S. Army Physicians' Memoir of Imprisonment by the Japanese 1942–*1945. McFarland & Co., Publishers. Jefferson, N C. and London. 1995.

U.S. News and World Report. Red Cross worker Marie Adams, World War II prisoner of the Japanese.<www.usnews. com> / July 24, 2006.

Gordon, Richard M. *Bataan, Corregidor, and the Death March in Retrospect* <http://home.pacbell.net/fbaldie/in_ retrospect.html>

ABOUT THE AUTHOR AND THIS BOOK

Gordon Sawyer will tell you his working career can best be described as journalist and promoter. But his avocation and hobby has been history, and especially the colorful and untold stories to be found in the mountains of Northeast Georgia.

He began his journalism career on the student newspaper at Georgia Tech. After service in the Navy in World War II, while doing graduate work in journalism and business at Emory University, he edited the student newspaper. He was a young reporter on the Atlanta Constitution under Ralph McGill before moving to Gainesville, Georgia, where he became executive secretary of the Georgia Poultry Federation, the legislative and promotion arm for the newly emerging broiler industry. Not surprisingly, that job also evolved to include editor of the Poultry Times, a trade newspaper. In 1960 he founded an advertising agency serving agribusiness and business-to-business clients, an enterprise that grew to gain national recognition.

It was after he retired from his agency in 1991 that he got serious about writing more than an occasional article about the unwritten history around him. Among his books have been *Northeast Georgia: A History* and *JAMES LONGSTREET:*

Before Manassas and After Appomattox, the story of Robert E. Lee's First Corps commander, who lost favor in the South after the Civil War and who is buried in Gainesville.

Richard Kidder was Gordon Sawyer's neighbor at Lanier Village Estates, a retirement resort on the shores of Lake Lanier. The historian in Sawyer told him this was a piece of World War II history that should be saved before it was too late. He did an article, then a presentation, and now this highly readable book, whose title serves as an outline for the story: *Richard Kidder. World War II. SURVIVOR. Manila to Bataan. To Corregidor. To Cabanatuan POW. To a Hell Ship. To Umeda Bunsho POW. To Tsuraga POW. And Home, Alive.*

Sawyer insists this is a story that should be recorded so that future generations can better understand the price many "everyday Americans" paid during World War II that we in the United States may live in freedom. As this was being written in 2007, Richard Kidder was 89 and Gordon Sawyer 81.

2139961